NELL W. MOHNEY

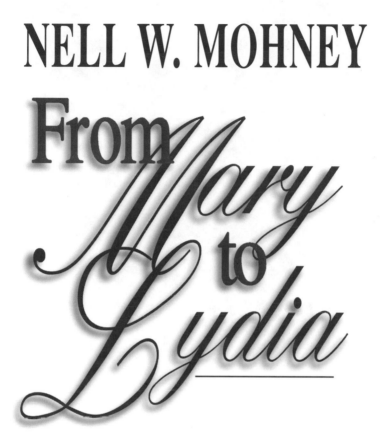

From Mary to Lydia

Letting New Testament Women Speak to Us

D0111852

DIMENSIONS
FOR LIVING

NASHVILLE

FROM MARY TO LYDIA
LETTING NEW TESTAMENT WOMEN SPEAK TO US

Library of Congress Cataloging-in-Publication Data

Mohney, Nell.
  From Mary to Lydia : letting New Testament women speak to us / Nell W. Mohney.
    p. cm.
  Includes bibliographical references.
  ISBN 0-687-09578-6 (alk. paper)
    1. Women in the Bible.   2. Bible. N.T.—Biography.   3. Christian women—Religious life.
I. Title.

BS2445 .M56 2002
220.9′2′082—dc21

                                                                          2001047825

02 03 04 05 06 07 08 09 10 11—10 9 8 7 6 5 4 3 2 1

MANUFACTURED IN THE UNITED STATES OF AMERICA

To the loving memory of

my dear friend Georgianna Webb,

who lost her battle against cancer

but never lost her faith in the living Christ

or her wonderful spirit of

Christian love, compassion, and laughter

CONTENTS

ACKNOWLEDGMENTS

T express heartfelt appreciation to:

My husband, Ralph W. Mohney Sr.,
who has given me daily encouragement for this project,
has been indefatigable at the computer,
and has told me funny stories when I was discouraged.

The personnel of the Reference and Fine Arts Departments
of the Hamilton County Bicentennial Library
for their willingness to do endless research at my request.

Two groups of friends,
the "Birthday Girls" and the
"Tuesday Floozies" (a facetious name for a diverse
but wonderful group of women)—who have regularly
checked on my progress and held me accountable.

INTRODUCTION

$\mathcal{T}$he women of the Bible have enriched my life tremendously. Not only have they helped me understand the culture of Bible times, but also they have made the Bible "come alive" for me. More important, God has spoken clearly and graphically to me through many of these women—women with whom we have much in common, despite the fact that they lived in a time and culture vastly different from our own. Some of these women are little known while others are more widely familiar, yet they all have valuable lessons to offer.

In this book, we focus on eight women of the New Testament and on the insights we can gain from them. Our journey takes us from Mary, the Mother of Jesus, who was ordained by God to bear the Messiah and who has something to teach us about finding our own calling or ministry, to Lydia, who was a successful career woman in a day when women were little more than chattel and who has something to say to women in the "marketplace" today. In between, we meet six interesting and dynamic women of the New Testament, including several unnamed women who played vital roles in the spread of Christianity in the early days of the church. Peter's wife, for instance, was never mentioned by name in the Bible; yet according to legend, she is believed to have been the inspirational and steadying force behind her dynamic and impetuous husband. She has much to teach us about how to really love a difficult man. Likewise, the woman with the issue of blood teaches us what it means to have bedrock faith despite difficult circumstances.

Because the scriptures often tell us little about some of these women, I have used the work of biblical scholars, research findings about the customs of the day, and my own imagination to fill in the "blank places." Each chapter begins with a "retelling" of a particular woman's story, followed by practical and spiritual lessons her story offers us today. A scripture text is provided so that you may read the biblical account for yourself. Every chapter ends with questions for reflection or discussion to help individuals or groups "dig a little deeper." A couple of chapters also include additional tools or exercises "for the journey ahead."

It is my prayer that you will listen carefully as God speaks specifically to some of your circumstances through these women of the New Testament.

1.

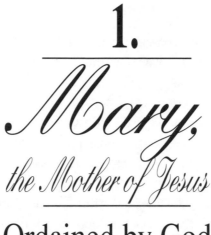

Mary, the Mother of Jesus

Ordained by God

Scripture Text: Luke 1:26-56; Matthew 1:18-25

And the angel said unto her, Fear not, Mary: for thou hast found favor with God.

—Luke 1:30 KJV

Mary's Story

Note: Some of the details in the following story, including Mary's age, are based on customs of the day; some are drawn from my own imagination. This creative retelling, I believe, allows us to see more clearly the courage it took for a teenager to obey God's command.

It was just two days before her fourteenth birthday, and Mary had never been filled with such joy. In fact, she had never known great pain or suffering in her short life—only joy. Now, joy was overflowing in each of her days.

Since she and Joseph had announced their engagement at the synagogue last month, each day was like a beautiful jewel made specifically for her. In the Jewish tradition of her day, engagement was a betrothal. The man and woman were considered married, except that the marriage was not consummated until after the wedding. The betrothal could last from six months to two years according to the wishes of the girl's parents.

Though Joseph was several years older than Mary, he had loved her since she was very young. He had not spoken of it until she was fourteen—the age when a girl was eligible for marriage. Like many of the girls in Nazareth, Mary had had a crush on the tall, muscular, and handsome Joseph since she was a child. Mary's parents liked him because he was a kind, responsible, and levelheaded man, as well as a devout, God-fearing Jew. He attended synagogue regularly and often was called on to read from the Torah. There were times when Mary's parents had wished that their exceptionally beautiful daughter could marry a wealthy man and be taken away from the hard work and poverty of the village of Nazareth. Yet if they had to choose between an unbeliever with material wealth and a poor man who devoutly believed in and served the true God, they always would choose the latter.

Then something happened. In the late afternoon, on her way to feed the animals, Mary was humming one of the psalms used in synagogue worship. Her heart was praising God when suddenly she sensed a presence with her. She stopped in her tracks upon seeing the bright light that beamed on her. Slowly, from the light, a presence appeared and a voice said, "Greetings, favored one! The Lord is with you" (Luke 1:28). Mary found herself drawing back in fear. Sensing Mary's fear, the angel spoke more gently: "Do not be afraid, Mary, for you have found favor with God. And now, you will conceive in your womb and bear a son, and you will name him Jesus. He will be great, and will be called the Son of the Most High, and the Lord God will give to him the throne of his ancestor David. He will reign over the house of Jacob forever, and of his kingdom there will be no end" (1:30-33).

Mary gasped for breath and, in total amazement and wide-eyed wonder, asked, "But how can this be since I have no husband yet?" (1:34, author's paraphrase).

The angel answered, "The Holy Spirit will come upon you, and the power of the Most High will overshadow you; therefore the child to be born will be holy; he will be called Son of God" (1:35).

The angel allowed Mary to catch her breath. Then, as if to reassure her, the angel told her that her cousin Elizabeth, in her old age, was six months with child, adding that "nothing is impossible with God" (1:37 NIV).

The young girl knew in her heart that the message she had heard was truly from God, so she bowed before the angel and replied, "Here am I, the servant of the Lord; let it be with me according to your word" (1:38). When she looked up, the bright light and the visitor were gone.

It took days for Mary to digest the message and to get the courage to tell her mother. As she had feared, her mother's reaction was swift and full of suspicion.

"How could you and Joseph consummate your marriage before the actual ceremony?" the distraught mother asked. "You bring dishonor to our family!"

"You know that neither Joseph nor I would do anything to bring dishonor to our families," Mary replied sadly. "No, we have never lain together, and the angel's appearance was real. I did not imagine it! He also told me that my cousin Elizabeth is with child in her old age and that with God, nothing is impossible. He suggested that I go visit Elizabeth."

"Well, at least we should see if he is right about Elizabeth," said the exasperated mother. "But, have you told Joseph yet?"

"No, but I will do it tonight," Mary said with dread in her voice. She knew only too well that Joseph had three options: to give her a writ of divorcement; to report her to the Sanhedrin, where they could stone her—for according to Jewish law, any woman, married or single, who had sex outside marriage could be stoned to death—or to marry her and accept total responsibility for the child.

Throughout this surprising episode, which turned her world upside down, Mary felt panic only once: when she told Joseph about the angel's appearance. As they walked alone in the garden that evening, Joseph gently put his arm around her shoulder and said, "Mary, you have been so quiet this past week. Is something wrong?"

As she turned toward him, she took a deep breath and blurted out the story of the angel's appearance. Joseph's face seemed frozen in amazement—and something else. Was it disbelief? Did Joseph actually believe that she had been unfaithful to him? Her heart was as heavy as a stone. Could she leave him like this for her visit to Elizabeth? But Joseph answered the question for her. He thought it would be a good idea since it would give them both an opportunity to think.

What was there to think about? wondered Mary. *Either the angel of God had appeared or not.* And Mary knew that she had heard the voice of God through the angel. Then why was her heart so troubled?

En route to the hill country to visit Elizabeth, Mary prayed that God would calm her spirit and guide her through her awesome responsibility. God answered both prayers. When Mary arrived at the home of Zechariah and Elizabeth, her cousin greeted her with these words: "Blessed are you among women, and blessed is the child you will bear! But why am I so favored, that the mother of my Lord should come to me? As soon as the sound of your greeting reached my ears, the baby in my womb leaped for joy. Blessed is she who has believed that what the Lord has said to her will be accomplished!" (Luke 1:42-45 NIV). Elizabeth knew! God had revealed the truth to Elizabeth. And Mary responded to Elizabeth's words with what we now call "the Magnificat" (Luke 1:46-55).

Meanwhile, back in Nazareth, the angel appeared to Joseph in a dream, saying: "Do not be afraid to take Mary as your wife, for the child conceived in her is from the Holy Spirit. She will bear a son, and you are to name him Jesus, for he will save his people from their sins" (Matthew 1:20-21).

When Mary returned, she and Joseph were married, and together they set about the awesome task of rearing the Son of God. Truly God is faithful! If we are obedient, God will provide the resources needed for the task we are asked to do.

What Can We Learn from Mary?

Lesson 1: We are all chosen (John 15:16), though not for the same tasks (Romans 12:4-8).

Although Mary's calling was far greater than that of any other Christian woman through the centuries, all of us are chosen and have a specific purpose to fulfill for God. In my life, this realization came in the summer of 1970 when my husband and I attended for the first time the Passion Play in Oberammergau, Germany. The play, which is the story of Christ's life, passion, death, and resurrection, was life changing for me.

The origin of the play goes back to the early seventeenth century, when the bubonic plague was sweeping through Europe. The small village of Oberammergau closed its borders to anyone from the outside. They wanted to avoid the plague at all costs. There was, however, a young man, Casper Schisler, who was working in Europe and was already infected with the plague. He wanted desperately to go home, and he succeeded in doing so by traveling unnoticed down steep mountain paths. He died shortly after reaching his home.

From the day of his death in April 1633, until October of the same year, there were eighty-two deaths from the plague registered in the small village. On October 26, the parish council went to the church and made a vow to God. If their village could be spared from any more deaths from the plague, they would perform a pageant on the life of Jesus and present it every ten years. From the time of the vow, no other villager died from the plague. The Bavarian people have kept their promise, and from 1633 to the present day, the Passion Play has been presented every ten years despite wars, difficulties, and some criticism.

In 1970, in the afternoon portion of the six-hour production, an eerie thing happened. At the time of day that Jesus would have been hanging on the cross, there was a sudden thunderstorm. The sky grew dark; there was lightning, loud thunder, and rain. Since the stage was not covered, the scene was realistically reminiscent of the gospel account of that day on Calvary so many years ago. The entire audience seemed gripped by the scene's power, and all five thousand of us walked out of the theater without a sound. Recognizing what Christ had done for me, I had never felt like such an unworthy disciple in my life. I couldn't stop crying.

Two days later, when we arrived in Vienna, Austria, my husband suggested that we go to Saint Stephens's Cathedral, which was near our hotel, and pray. In my prayers, as I repeated my feelings of unworthiness, the words of Jesus from John 15:16 rushed into my mind with such force that I knew Christ was saying them to me—and to all who call themselves believers: "Ye have not chosen me, but I have chosen you, and ordained you, that ye should go and bring forth fruit" (KJV). Beside that passage in my Bible I have written these words: "My ordination: June 25, 1970." Whenever I am feeling inadequate or unworthy, I remember my ordination and seek to go forth in his power.

Lesson 2: God never chooses us for a task without providing the necessary resources to see us through.

God did more than choose Mary and Joseph to fulfill his grand design; he provided all the resources they needed to see them through the task. For example, God took the fear and doubt from Joseph's mind by appearing to him in a dream. Likewise, God allowed Elizabeth to understand what had happened to Mary so that Elizabeth might serve as an encourager at a critical time in the life of the teenage girl. I also believe that Mary received a special measure of courage for this most important of all tasks.

I know firsthand of God's gracious provision. After giving me the dream of ministering to others through writing, speaking, and teaching, God confirmed the call through increasing and diverse invitations, as well as through people—sometimes unexpected ones—who encouraged me and pointed the way. When I was trying to discern whether God wanted me to accept speaking engagements from business and professional groups or to speak only to Christian groups, my seatmate on a lengthy flight was a well-known Christian speaker. In the course of our conversation, she mentioned that she had prayed to be allowed to speak to secular as well as to Christian groups. But no invitations from the former had come. Suddenly, bells went off in my mind and heart. My prayer for guidance had been answered, and from a most unlikely source. God was calling me to speak to both Christians and nonbelievers. Likewise, whenever I needed encouragement or affirmation, a telephone call, a note of appreciation, or a very positive evaluation form made me aware of what was most meaningful in my writing and speaking. If we are willing to be used, and if we do our part in preparation, God will provide the needed resources. Trust God on this one!

Lesson 3: The closer we walk in daily fellowship with Christ, the easier it is to trust his call to us.

Obviously, Christ had not come to the earth when Mary received her call. She was, however, utterly devoted to God; and this was evident in her personal morality, her joyful living, her knowledge of the scriptures (she was singing one of the psalms on her way to feed the animals), and her regular attendance at synagogue worship. Thus, when the call came from God, Mary recognized it immediately.

One of the persons who seemed to have heard God's call most clearly was Dr. E. Stanley Jones, renowned missionary to India and evangelist to America. In 1955, he came to speak for a week in the church in which my husband was pastor. Dr. Jones had long been my spiritual mentor through the books he had written. Many authors tell us what we ought to do or believe, yet they don't give us practical ways to accomplish this. Dr. Jones seemed to know the problems we all encounter on our journeys and gave us step-by-step ways to handle them. His real-life illustrations are like well-focused pictures we can hang on the walls of our minds. One picture is, indeed, worth more than a thousand words. All these years later, I still can recall many of his illustrations.

While preaching in our church, Dr. Jones told of going to India as a young man. There he saw so many things that needed to be done that he took his eyes off Jesus and saw only the problems and his limited resources. The result was a complete nervous breakdown. As he described this period in vivid detail, he reminded us to walk closely and daily with Christ, our true source. Using the words of the chorus "Turn Your Eyes upon Jesus" by Helen H. Lemmel (1950), Dr. Jones suggested that as we look into the face of Jesus,

> The things of earth will grow strangely dim
> In the light of his glory and grace.

The world in which we live today is so secularized that its busyness and distractions often prevent our hearing and heeding God's call. We must be intentional about simplifying our lives and having a daily quiet time. During this time, as we read the scriptures, think about them, and pray, we are much more likely to hear our call when it comes.

Digging a Little Deeper

1. Read Luke 1:26-38. Of all the women living in the world at that time, why do you think God chose Mary?
2. We know that because God gives all people freedom of choice, not everyone chooses to heed God's call. Certainly not all the people of the Bible heeded God's message, including Adam and Eve (see Genesis 2:15-25 and chap. 3) and Jonah (see the book of Jonah, chaps. 1–4). Why, then, do you think Mary answered so quickly and positively? See Luke 1:38.
3. What do you think you would have done if you had received the same call as Mary when you were a teenager? Why?
4. Read Luke 1:42-45. How did God use Elizabeth to confirm the angel's message?
5. For Mary, perhaps the most difficult part of accepting God's call must have been wondering what Joseph would do. According to Jewish law, what three choices did he have? How did God prepare Joseph for his decision? Read Matthew 1:20-21.
6. Have there been times in your life when you felt that God was calling you to a particular task or a certain vocation? Did you heed the call? Discuss.
7. What distracts you from hearing God's messages? What might sensitize you to the messages of God? How does walking in daily fellowship with Jesus Christ help us hear God's call? What does that mean to you?

2.
Peter's Wife

She Inspired Her Husband

Scripture Text: **Matthew 8:14-15; 1 Corinthians 9:5**

When Jesus came into Peter's house, he saw Peter's mother-in-law lying in bed with a fever. He touched her hand and the fever left her, and she got up and began to wait on him.

—Matthew 8:14-15 NIV

Her Story

Note: The following dialogue is from my imagination. The Bible has only two specific references to Peter's wife (Matthew 8:14-15 and 1 Corinthians 9:5), and neither gives her name. For readability's sake, I have chosen to use a name, Bernice, which was a common name of the day.

Peter's wife, Bernice, was running frantically from street to street in Jerusalem, looking for her husband. Then she spotted her friend Elizabeth, who came to her and said, "What is it, Bernice? You look so troubled!"

"It's Peter. Have you seen him? I *must* find him," Bernice said as she continued to glance in all directions.

As Elizabeth placed an arm around her friend's shoulder to comfort her, she replied, "He must surely be at Golgotha—at that terrible crucifixion. After all, Peter was one of Jesus' closest disciples."

"Yes, he loved the Master with a deep devotion and followed him without reservation. But that is the problem. I just heard that while Jesus was being taken from the Sanhedrin to Pilate's palace, Peter sat outside the palace in the courtyard and denied that he even knew Jesus (Matthew 26:69-76). I can't imagine what might have happened! But I am sure of one thing: When he realizes what he has done, he will be inconsolable; and I am not sure what he will do. You know how impetuous he is."

"Yes, I know," said Elizabeth. "We have often wondered how you could live with such a difficult man."

Bernice's eyes softened as she said quietly, "I love him. That's it. I simply love him. He *is* opinionated, impatient, impetuous, and full of bravado, but he is a good man in his heart—and lovable. Oh, I'll admit that before Peter met Jesus, we had some difficult days. I was so frustrated that, at times, I was almost ready to give up. But Jesus changed Peter. He saw beyond the bluster and bluff to Peter's possibilities. He is the one who first called him Peter, not Simon (Matthew 16:15-18). Peter sought to live up to that name, which means 'the rock.' He became calmer and steadier and far more focused."

As Bernice looked directly into Elizabeth's eyes, she admitted, "Jesus changed me, too. I grew to be far gentler and calmer, and I also became a follower." She paused a moment. Then, as if pulling herself back from memory to reality, she continued, "That's why I *must* find Peter."

Suddenly the sky became dark. There was thunder and lightning. In one of the lightning flashes, both women spotted Peter. He was sitting alone on a grassy knoll across from Golgotha, sobbing. Bernice ran to his side.

The big fisherman put his muscular arms around her and said, "Oh, Bernice, when he needed me most, I denied that I even knew him. There was a mob. It was noisy and confusing, and I was terrified; but I can't believe that I did it. I didn't act like a 'rock'—more like a despicable worm."

Bernice replied in a clear, calm voice, "Peter, he has already for-given you. Do you remember the time when you asked how often we ought to forgive? You suggested that seven times seven would be far more than the 'eye for an eye and a tooth for a tooth,' which is usually practiced. But Jesus said, 'No, Peter, not seven times but seventy times seven' (Matthew 18:21-22). In other words, more than we can even count. He has already for-given you, Peter, and he has removed it as far as the east is from the west. What we can do for him now is carry on the work he began."

"Bernice, you always keep my thinking straight. Thank you for coming to be with me in my shame—and for loving me all these years."

At that moment there was a loud clap of thunder and a strong voice from the body on the cross: "Father, into your hands I commend my spirit" (Luke 23:46). Bowing their heads as they clung to each other, Peter and his wife determined individually to be all that Christ believed them to be. Peter whispered to Bernice, "I will serve him as long as I have breath."

What Can We Learn from Peter's Wife?

Lesson 1: The sum of one plus one is greater than the number two.

As I have observed married couples through the years, I have come to believe that if they individually love Christ, love each other, and seek to enhance each other's strengths and to balance their own weaknesses, then the strength of the couple is far greater than the strength of the two individuals. This is synergy. For a couple, this synergy is made up of love, commitment, self-acceptance, awareness of the spouse's needs, and a willingness to be adjustable.

Though the Bible tells us nothing about Peter's wife, we can learn a great deal about her—and about her relationship with her husband—by considering what we know about Peter. We know that Jesus chose Peter as his successor. After Peter confessed that Jesus was the Christ (Matthew 16:16), Jesus changed Simon's name to Peter, which means "rock." In Matthew 16:18-19, Jesus declares: "Thou art Peter, and upon this rock I will build my church; and the gates of hell shall not prevail against it. And I will give unto thee the keys of the kingdom of heaven" (KJV). Jesus was resting his Kingdom on the Gibraltar of Peter's faith, and two thousand years later, the gates of hell have not prevailed against it.

Even so, like all of us, Peter was a "Christian under construction." Before he became Jesus' rock, he promised more than he could deliver. In the Upper Room, when Jesus announced that one of the twelve would betray him, Peter declared: "Lord, I am ready to go with you to prison and to death" (Luke 22:33 NIV). Yet Peter denied his Lord three times (Luke 22:56-62). And there were times when Peter lost his nerve—such as the time that he wanted to walk on the water, and Jesus told him to come. As long as Peter kept his eyes on Jesus, he did fine; but when he looked at the swirling waters below, he began to sink (Matthew 14:25-33). Peter also often acted before he thought. Most scholars believe that it was Peter who cut off the right ear of one of the soldiers who came to arrest Jesus (Luke 22:49-51). It was such an impetuous, and thus unpredictable, man to whom Bernice was married; and such a man would not be easy to live with day after day.

At first glance, it may seem likely that Bernice had to do all the giving in their relationship—that Peter was a selfish "taker." I once attended the seminar "Happiness in Marriage" led by Dr. Larry Crabb, a Christian author and speaker. He said that a tick on a dog is a taker. The tick has no concern for the needs of the dog. Its only interest is how much blood it can get from the dog. Some people, he said, are like that. And if both marriage partners are takers, it is disastrous. That, he said, is like having two ticks and no dog!

Peter was no such taker. He may have been impetuous and impatient and difficult to live with at times, but he also was a natural leader and a very lovable person. For example, he was in Jesus' inner circle of friends: Peter, James, and John. At the request of Jesus, the three of them were with him on the Mount of Transfiguration (Matthew 17:1-9) and in the Garden of Gethsemane (Matthew 26:36-38). Furthermore, as we've already noted, it was Peter who first identified Jesus as the Son of God: "You are the Christ, the Son of the living God" (Matthew 16:16 NIV). Jesus said that his church would be built on Peter's affirmation. Peter also served as spokesman for the disciples, indicating that they not only liked him but also recognized his leadership ability. He was creative and spontaneous in his thinking— not linear. People like that may be unpredictable, but they are never boring. They are stimulating to the thinking of others and simply fun to be around.

So in the marriage of Peter and Bernice, there must have been a great deal of give and take. In light of 1 Corinthians 9:5 ("Do we not have the right to be accompanied by a believing wife, as do the other apostles and the brothers of the Lord"), we can assume that Peter's wife traveled with him much of the time, especially after Jesus' death. Yet there were many responsibilities and duties that took Peter away from her. Bernice must have had great self-acceptance; in other words, she must have liked herself. She must have had enough interests, friends, and dreams to allow her to enjoy her life whether Peter was fishing commercially, spending time with Jesus, or leading the disciples. An insecure wife who clung tenaciously to her husband and resented his every absence would have made Peter's accomplishments impossible—and her own life miserable.

Most scholars believe that Peter used his wife as the model for his description of the Christian wife found in 1 Peter 3:1-6. When he spoke of "the unfading beauty of a gentle and quiet spirit" (v. 4 NIV), he surely was describing the woman who had brought balance and calmness into his own bombastic personality. Yes, I am sure that Peter and Bernice complemented each other—each affirming the other's strengths and compensating for his or her own weaknesses. No doubt this was especially true after they met Jesus.

When I think of such a couple in contemporary life, I think of Ruth and Billy Graham. As a feature writer for a newspaper over a period of twenty-two years, I have interviewed Dr. Graham on three occasions. In one of the interviews, he said that early in the marriage, Ruth traveled with him. After the children came, however, she felt that her ministry was to preside over a safe and secure and warm environment in which to rear young Christians. They both agreed that God had called Billy to be an evangelist. But Ruth believed that her call was equally as strong. She was no insecure wife! She was—and is—a confident, competent, committed Christian who continues to listen to God's call on her own life. Through the years, she has accompanied Billy on such occasions as presidential inaugurations, National Prayer Breakfasts, and visits with kings and queens. In between Evangelistic Crusades, Billy has been a devoted husband and father to his family in Montreat, North Carolina. Years ago I read a magazine article about Ruth Graham. The author asked how she felt about Billy being away so often. Her reply was classic: that she would rather be married to Billy Graham for one day of the year than to any other man that she knew for 365 days a year.

I'm confident that Bernice must have felt the same way about

Peter. In the book *All the Women of the Bible,* Herbert Lockyer tells a poignant legend in church tradition that claims Peter and his wife died together, one after the other. According to the legend, Peter comforted her with these words: "Remember the Lord" (Grand Rapids: Zondervan, 1967, p. 220). This, of course, is not in scripture, but I have always liked the thought of their being together at the end. They probably were imprisoned together in Manertine Prison in Rome, and they would have been able to comfort each other before their executions. I like to think also that they were able to greet the Lord again together.

Perhaps the closest we come to heaven or hell on earth is a really good or a really bad marriage. It was Edgar A. Guest who wrote "It takes a heap o' livin' in a house t' make it home" (from "Home," in *Collected Verse of Edgar A. Guest,* Chicago: The Reilly & Lee Co., 1934). That kind of living involves love, understanding, respect, flexibility, willingness to change, and commitment to Jesus Christ on the part of both spouses. The marriage of Peter and his wife shows us that the equation is not really one plus one, but one plus one plus "The One."

Lesson 2: All of us will encounter difficult people along life's journey, and we should be prepared to respond—not react—to them.

Is there someone in your life who really "bugs" you? I am not talking about the people you seldom see or don't even know—for example, people who cut in front of you in traffic, people who elbow their way to the front of a long line in a cafeteria, people who are loud and obnoxious in a quiet restaurant, people who act as if they know it all, people who won't be decisive about a dinner invitation, a service technician who promises to come at a particular time and doesn't come (and doesn't call). These people may irritate you, but you can usually handle it.

The difficult people I am talking about are those to whom we have to relate on a regular basis: colleagues at work, employers, employees, former spouses—even spouses, parents, children, and other relatives. Sometimes I have facetiously wondered if the reason there are so many suicides at Christmastime is that all those difficult relatives get together in small spaces to celebrate the holidays. Seriously, at one time or another we all have to cope with difficult people.

Joyce Landorf calls such people "irregular people" in her book by the same name (Waco, Tex.: Word Publishing, 1982). Her title comes from a TV drama based on the award-winning book *Summer of My German Soldier* by Bette Green (New York: Laurel-Leaf Library, 1993). The story centers around a small southern town during World War II. The principal characters are a young German prisoner, who escapes from jail in an Arkansas town, and Patty Bergan, the twelve-year-old girl who accidentally discovers him.

Patty befriends the prisoner and hides him in the playroom above her father's barn. Later, when he feels he is putting Patty in jeopardy, the prisoner tries to escape; but he is shot down by the FBI. When Patty's father confronts her, he releases a stream of verbal abuses in a voice choked with hatred. He tells her that he never loved her because she reminds him of his mother, whom he hated. After saying that he has to keep her in his house until she is eighteen, he ends the tirade by growling in contempt that she is dead to him.

Shaken and shattered, the young girl runs across town to the large black woman, Ruth, who was the cook and housekeeper in the Bergan home until she was fired for defending Patty too often. Ruth, as she comforts the girl, tells her that when she goes shopping and sees something marked "Irregular," she knows she won't have to pay so much for it. Then she says something to this effect: You've got yourself some irregular folks, and you've been paying more'n top dollar for them. So don't go awishing for what ain't nevah gonna be (p. 192). Ruth tells Patty to straighten up her shoulders because she is a creature of God and a person who matters in the world. She tells her to have personal pride and never to let her shoulders or her soul slope again.

When I read those wise words, I thought of all the people who go through life trying to win approval from the difficult persons who will not, or cannot, show them approval. These difficult people often display similar characteristics—characteristics such as manipulative behavior, insensitivity to the needs and feelings of others, an unwillingness or inability to apologize, defensiveness, inflexibility, self-pity, a certainty that they are right (and thus a tendency to blame others for failure), and an unwillingness to examine their own thoughts and behavior patterns. Unfortunately, many people paralyze their own chances for happiness by staying bound to such difficult persons by hatred or resentment.

What then, are some ways that we, as Christians, should respond to such persons?

First, we can look honestly at ourselves to see whether or not we are one of them. Are we making someone else's life miserable? Jesus asked, "Why do you see the speck in your neighbor's eye, but do not notice the log in your own eye?" (Matthew 7:3).

Looking back, the town in which I grew up seemed to have had more gossip than any other place I have lived. Perhaps this was because our town was small and we lived in close proximity to one another. In those years, most women didn't work outside the home; hence, they got together often and, perhaps naturally, discussed their neighbors. In fairness, I must say that these people were always there for one another if there was sickness, death, or any difficulties.

Most of the gossip was harmless, but it simply was not a good use of time. There was, however, one woman who added cruelty to her stories. For some reason, she didn't like an out-of-town couple who had moved next door to her. She started some rumors that later proved to be untrue. But in the meantime, those rumors deeply hurt the wife and negatively affected the husband's business.

After the truth became known, our minister preached a memorable sermon on the use of the tongue, based on James 3:1-8. That morning as I walked out of church, I was shocked to overhear the woman who had started the rumor say to the minister: "That was a great sermon. I only wish my sister could have heard it."

Scottish poet Robert Burns, on seeing an elegantly dressed woman in church who was unaware that a louse was crawling down her hair, wrote these lines:

> O wad some Power the giftie gie us
> To see ourseles as ithers see us!
> (from "To a Louse," *The Complete Poetical Works of Burns,* Boston: Houghton Mifflin, 1897)

In order to see our own faults, we must honestly evaluate ourselves every so often, asking questions such as these: Do I try to control situations? Do I criticize others too often? Do I boast of my accomplishments and turn people off? Do I interrupt when others are speaking? Whenever we ask these and other pertinent questions, we should do so in a time of prayer. If we are open to God's leadership, we will become more and more aware of the "logs in our own eyes."

Second, we can take time for thoughtful and prayerful consideration of the conflict and then change what *we* can change. This may involve a confrontation—or care-frontation, as I like to call it. In short, it involves looking for opportunities to resolve conflicts peacefully.

A care-frontation means that we carefully choose our timing before we lovingly approach the other person. Even as children, we sensed when we should show our parents our report cards. As adults, we instinctively know when to talk with a friend about a concern or with a spouse about a purchase. Likewise, we should choose well the time to discuss a conflict—never when you or the other person is angry or hungry or under extreme stress. In particular, we must be respectful of the other person's feelings and careful to attack the *issue,* never the other person. We should avoid using the pronoun "you," as when saying, "*You* are responsible for this," or "Look what a mess *you* have made!" People become defensive when they are personally attacked. Instead, we should say something such as, "*We* seem to have a conflict here. Let's see how *we* can handle it," or "*I* feel angry when our family reunions end in conflict and chaos. How can *we* change that?" People can deal with our feelings more easily than they can handle our attacks upon them.

Of course, we must accept the fact that our difficult person may never change. We can't change another person. The only persons we can change, with the help of God through Jesus Christ, are ourselves. There comes a time when we must accept what is, rather than wish for what will never be.

Third, we can talk over the situation with a wise person who can give objective advice. For me, a wise person is a person with a strong Christian faith who has a track record of making wise decisions. Usually this is a person who is older or more experienced than I. If the hurts are too deep or the pain is too fresh, we may need to see a professional counselor. For me, an acceptable counselor is always one who has good credentials in counseling and is a person of faith.

Fourth, when seeking to resolve conflict, we always should approach the other person with creative goodwill and forgiveness. Maybe we can't honestly forgive, but we can ask God to forgive the person through us. Remember that we always will be bound to a person we have not forgiven. Forgiveness is one of the most difficult things to give—especially if the hurt is deep. Yet, Jesus' insistence upon forgiveness indicates that we can never be free and whole if we lock ourselves in the prison of bitter memories or wallow in yesterday's pain. Forgiveness involves recognizing and facing the wrong that has been done to us, acknowledging any part we had in causing the wrong, and then "letting go and letting God" heal us of the hurt. All the "king's horses" cannot force us to forgive someone. We must *choose* to forgive. Otherwise, our hearts and souls become shriveled in bitterness.

I once saw the Christmas television drama "Timepiece" (1996), starring Richard Thomas and James Earl Jones. It is the story of a young, happily married couple and the small daughter whom they adored. A man who hated the husband threw a bomb through the little girl's bedroom window while she slept. She died from asphyxiation before her parents discovered the fire. The couple's hatred of the perpetrator and their own feelings of guilt destroyed the closeness in their marriage and robbed them of joy. It was only when their priest persuaded them to take Christmas gifts to the imprisoned man's wife and children that they were set free to begin the process of forgiveness.

In the book *Forgive and Forget* (San Francisco: Harper & Row, 1984), Lewis B. Smedes suggests that love is the power behind forgiveness—not love as a soft and fuzzy sentiment, but love as a powerful force. A part of that love, he says, is self-respect. This means setting limits to the abuse that we will accept from thoughtless or cruel people, even if we love them. Love, he says, also respects other people as human beings of worth because they are made in the image of God. Those hurtful people are not just lumps of degenerate corruption. There is more to them than the hurt they inflicted on us. Respect for them eventually will allow forgiveness of them. Only God can affect that forgiveness, but we have to be willing to open our hearts to allow forgiveness.

Fifth, after confessing our own mistakes, we need to forgive ourselves. It constantly amazes me to see people who believe God has forgiven them, and yet they won't forgive themselves. In so doing, they inflict unnecessary punishment on themselves and miss the joy of living.

The book *God's Smuggler* (New York: New American Library, 1967) tells the story of Brother Andrew, the courageous Dutch missionary who went "underground" in the Communist countries in 1955. There he distributed Bibles and encouragement to Christians behind the iron curtain. Yet with all his good works, he couldn't forgive himself for something that happened during World War II. His battalion had inadvertently killed some children. He sought God's forgiveness and believed that he had received it. Yet, he simply couldn't forgive himself. Years later, he went back to the town, and on the spot where the incident had happened stood a playground. Suddenly a little girl left her playmates, ran over to him, and, looking up, gave him a big smile and a hug around his knees. It was as if God had sent a special child to confirm that he was forgiven and should forgive himself. From that day forward, Andrew fulfilled his ministry with greater freedom and joy.

Sixth, we need to remember that God didn't cause the conflict, but he can use it. Like an oyster uses an irritant to create a pearl, God can use our irritants to teach us patience and enable us to grow toward maturity. The story of Joseph in the Old Testament is a beautiful example (see Genesis 37, 39–50). After Joseph reveals his identity to his brothers in chapter 42, they are afraid of what he might do to them. Then, in chapter 50, he says these wonderful words: "You intended to harm me, but God intended it for good to accomplish what is now being done, the saving of many lives" (v. 20 NIV).

Finally, whatever the outcome of the particular situation or relationship, we can be true to who we are—created by God, redeemed by Christ, and empowered by the Holy Spirit—and who we are called to be. We cannot allow our difficult person to dictate how we feel or how we will react. When Jesus coped with a difficult person, Judas, he did everything he could to make a difference in their relationship. He loved Judas, taught him, served him. But when Judas left in the act of betrayal, Jesus didn't beg him to stay or change his own mission because of it. Instead, he forgave Judas while remaining focused on his mission.

When dealing with difficult people, each of us has a choice. Despite our circumstances, we can choose not to react to a difficult person but to respond proactively, so that we can be all that God created us to be.

Digging a Little Deeper

1. What were some of Simon Peter's characteristics that might have made him difficult to live with? Read Matthew 16:21-25, Luke 22:33-34, Matthew 26:69-75, and Matthew 14:25-31. Discuss the personal characteristics of Peter found in each scripture reference.
2. Read Matthew 16:13-19, Acts 2:38-41, Acts 3:1-10, Acts 4:13-21, Acts 5:14-15, and Acts 12:1-17. Recall some of Peter's good qualities displayed before the Resurrection, and discuss the power that became his after the Resurrection.
3. Many scholars believe that Peter was describing his own wife in 1 Peter 3:1-6. Based on these verses, what do you think she was like? How do you believe she might have coped with difficult circumstances?
4. Do you have difficult persons in your life? How have you coped with them in the past? How has your Christian faith influenced your behavior? What changes might you need to make in the way you deal with these persons?
5. Evaluate yourself honestly. Are you ever a difficult person to someone else? Discuss. How might an awareness of your own faults be of help to you in dealing with the difficult people in your life?

3.

Mary and Martha

Right Brain, Left Brain Thinkers

Scripture Text: **Luke 10:38-42; John 11:17-29**

As Jesus and his disciples were on their way, he came to a village where a woman named Martha opened her home to him. She had a sister called Mary, who sat at the Lord's feet listening to what he said.
—Luke 10:38-39 NIV

Mary and Martha's Story

There was something about the late afternoon that made Martha pensive. Maybe it was the fact that most of the necessary chores of the day were finished and there was time for reflective thought. It was Jesus who had taught her the importance of taking time for reflection and prayer. There will always be mundane tasks necessary for living in this world. That is life. But of what value is life if there is no meaning?

As Martha walked down the lane from their fruit orchard, where she had picked dates and apples to add to the dinner meal, she thought of two incidents when Jesus had taught the same truths that he had taught Mary. Just ahead of her was the shaded courtyard of the spacious two-story stone house left to her by her late husband, who had been known as Simon the leper. Since his death, the house had been home also for her younger brother, Lazarus, and her sister, Mary. Their willingness to move into her home had eased some of her grief and had made the house seem less lonely. It was around the time of their move that the three of them had first heard Jesus speak. His words had been like arrows, piercing each of their hearts. Yet instead of death, those arrows had brought new life and meaning.

Martha recalled the time when Jesus and his disciples stayed in their home for the first time. Immediately she had been able to tell that the cool courtyard, good food, and loving atmosphere brought relaxation to the weary travelers. Their frequent visits confirmed that she had the gift of hospitality. She believed that an orderly, pleasant, and attractive environment helped people relax and think clearly. However, even before Jesus' first visit, she had secretly suspected that her desire for cleanliness and busyness had become an obsession. Still, perfection in homemaking was so much a part of her life that she didn't know how to order life any other way.

By now, Martha had reached the courtyard. As she sat down on a bench to enjoy the coolness of the day, she remembered the time when she had had to face her obsession. Lazarus had been with Jesus and the disciples in Jerusalem. Martha had not expected them back that day; but in the late afternoon, her brother came ahead of the others to report that all thirteen of them would be there for dinner and an overnight visit. That had thrown Martha into "stress overdrive." Although she had servants, she had been overwhelmed by all the planning and directing that would be necessary to prepare for the unexpected visit.[1]

---

[1] All affluent people of the day had servants. In his book *All the Women of the Bible*, Herbert Lockyer writes that the spacious house, the fact that Martha could provide large meals repeatedly, and the expensive perfume, with which Mary anointed Jesus (see Mark 14:3-9 and John 12:8), speak of affluence.

As she sat on the courtyard bench, Martha thought of that visit and wondered how she ever could have burst into a roomful of men and her sister while Jesus was teaching. She hadn't even waited for him to ask what was wrong. She had interrupted his teaching and, in irritation, had blurted out, "Lord, don't you care that my sister has left me to do the work by myself? Tell her to help me!" (Luke 10:40 NIV).

Even then, Martha's cheeks reddened as she thought of this indiscretion. Actually, Mary helped the servants any time she was asked. What Martha really had been feeling at the time was self-pity. She, too, had wanted to listen to Jesus' teaching. Even in the short time she had known him, she had developed an insatiable thirst for the truths proclaimed by the Master. She could have said what the poet Gamaliel Bradford said years later: "My one unchanged obsession, wheresoe'er my feet have trod, / Is a keen, enormous, haunting, never-sated thirst for God" (from "God" in _Shadow Verses_; New Haven: Yale University Press, 1920).

Martha recalled Jesus' rebuke: "Martha, Martha, you are worried and upset about many things, but only one thing is needed. Mary has chosen what is better, and it will not be taken away from her" (Luke 10:41-42 NIV). Jesus had spoken in such kindness that Martha had not felt "put down" and Mary had not felt humiliated. After dinner that evening, as she had replayed the scene in her mind, Martha had determined that Jesus was saying that her pretentious meals were unnecessary. Simple fare expressed hospitality and could keep her from becoming irritated and anxious. It had been a turning point in her life.

By then, the sun was beginning to go down behind the Judean hills. It was almost time for dinner, but Martha had been freed from perfectionism—from the compulsion to prepare an absolutely perfect meal at an exact time. So she allowed herself to cherish the memory of the time when Jesus had raised Lazarus from the dead after he had been in the tomb for four days (John

11:1-45). Both she and Mary had been overcome with grief after their brother's death. But when they heard that Jesus was coming, they reacted very differently—each being true to her temperament. Martha, the pragmatic hostess, had dried her eyes and had gone to greet him. Mary, the sensitive mystic, had been unable to control her grief and had stayed behind, keeping inside.

When Martha greeted Jesus, she had expressed what she and her sister both had felt: "Lord, if you had been here, my brother would not have died" (John 11:21 NIV). And when Jesus said, "Your brother will rise again," she had answered, "I know he will rise again in the resurrection at the last day" (vv. 23-24 NIV).

Suddenly Martha felt shivers running up and down her spine, just as she had the day of their miracle when Jesus had said to her, "*I* am the resurrection and the life. He who believes in me will live, even though he dies; and whoever lives and believes in me will never die. Do you believe this?" (vv. 25-26 NIV, emphasis added). The words in reply had rushed from her lips: "Yes, Lord, I believe that you are the Christ, the Son of God, who was to come into the world" (v. 27 NIV). When she had uttered those words, she had known that she was in the presence of the Almighty.

Both Martha and Mary had been with Jesus when he raised Lazarus from the dead and restored him to family life—a magnificent miracle that brought many townspeople into the Christian faith.

A deep sense of peace settled over Martha as she rose from the bench and stood in the courtyard. She walked slowly into the kitchen where servants had the evening meal ready—except for washing the fruit she had picked. What Martha felt inside was "the better part" that Jesus had mentioned on the day of her rebuke. Thankfully, she realized how she had grown in faith and understanding.

What Can We Learn from Mary and Martha?

Lesson 1: Members of the same family think and feel differently, yet all have special God-given abilities.

Mary and Martha had very different personalities. Martha was a left brain thinker. In other words, she thought in words and numbers, which meant she was practical, pragmatic. As the oldest child, she accepted responsibility easily. She was a "take charge" person with organizational skills. When there was work to be done, she attacked it with energetic zeal. Her bustling busyness probably made others uncomfortable.

In contrast to her older sister, Mary was a right brain thinker. That is, she thought in pictures and was very creative. She wanted time to think, to learn, to reflect. She probably didn't enjoy housework. Yet, she was indebted to her sister's organizational skills, which resulted in a pleasant and orderly household. Because of Martha's left brain tendencies, Mary had time to cultivate her spirit.

My own grandmothers were much like Mary and Martha. My maternal grandmother was a left brain thinker. As a widow with eleven children, Grandmother Ferree ran a "tight ship." Her house was like a busy beehive—with Grandmother as "queen bee." She assigned and directed all the chores, and everyone, including guests, had chores to do during the day. I always felt guilty when I was tempted to stop and play—or even to swing in the hammock. Thankfully, late afternoons and evenings in her home were much more relaxed, with games being played both inside and outside. Although I enjoyed being with my cousins at her home, the ambiance of the household was "bustling busyness," which made me uneasy as a child. In retrospect, I realize that if Grandmother Ferree had not been a left brain thinker, she never could have managed such a large household alone. A less organized person would have created chaos.

My paternal grandmother was a right brain thinker. Grandmother Webb's household was never highly organized, yet it was not chaotic. Having only three children, which was a small family in her day, she had time to have several cousins visit at once. We—including Grandmother—took nature hikes, created stories as we sat around the fire, sang, and laughed a lot. As a child, it was fun to go to Grandmother Webb's house.

Do I think one way is better than the other? Perhaps I once did but not anymore. As an adult, I've recalled Grandmother Ferree's organizational skills with appreciation for her love of order. Her household would have been unmanageable without these skills. Indeed, I learned so much from both of my grandmothers.

In the account of Jesus' visit with Mary and Martha, found in Luke 10:38-42, it seems to me that Jesus was seeking to help each of the sisters realize that we are called to be "whole brain" thinkers. When he rebuked Martha for allowing the necessary but mundane tasks of life to become dominant (vv. 41-42), he was saying, in effect, that her anxiety and worry were strangling the eternal part of herself out of existence. If she continued in this way, she would become even more anxious and irritable, more demanding of others, and less content or satisfied. As a result, life would become meaningless.

The Anglo-Saxon root word for *worry* means "to strangle." If you ever have been worried about something (and we all have), you know that this meaning is right on target. The spiritual life is literally strangled out of us when we are upset and worried. Our worries reveal much about our priorities in life.

In the book *The Workbook on Coping as Christians* (Nashville: The Upper Room, 1988), Maxie Dunnam writes: "Worry frets about a problem, concern solves the problem" (p. 36). Worry, on the one hand, is like a broken record. Your thoughts go round and round in the same groove and can't get "unstuck," preventing you from taking action. Concern, on the other hand, is seeing the problem with clear perspective and then taking positive action to correct it or turn it loose. "Whole brain" thinking enables us to move from worry to proactive concern.

Like her sister, Mary needed to be reminded of the importance of balance in life. When she could not control her feelings of grief after her brother had died, Jesus sent for her to dry her eyes and join them (John 11:20-30). He was saying, in effect, that faith is not a feeling. Rather, it is the bedrock _belief_ that Jesus is "the resurrection and the life" (v. 25 NIV). When we allow feelings to be dominant in our lives, we limit our capacity to have faith. It is the presence of Jesus, through the Holy Spirit, that gives us the balance we need—the ability to catch God's dreams (right brain activity) and the skills and persistence to put them into action (left brain activity). Under Jesus' direction, we become whole brain thinkers capable of having the abundant life of which he spoke: "I am come that they might have life, and that they might have it more abundantly" (John 10:10 KJV).

Martin Luther King Jr. was a whole brain thinker. His right brain tendencies were evident even from his early years when his belief that God wanted a peaceful, discrimination-free world sparked a dream within him. He became an ordained minister when he was nineteen and soon began to persuade others of his dream. His left brain thinking was evident when he later mobilized African Americans in nonviolent resistance. He was only thirty when the Civil Rights Act was signed, and at age thirty-five, he was the youngest person ever to receive the Nobel Peace Prize. Four years later, his life was over, but his legacy lived on.

Most of us know what it's like to have a dream. Unfortunately, few of us ever follow our dream, citing excuses such as "I'm too old," "I'm too young," "Nobody will listen to me," "I'm too shy," "I don't have enough money to get started," or "I'm a low-energy person." I am convinced that when God gives us a dream, God also provides the resources necessary to accomplish that dream. Our job is to use both parts of our minds to see the options and to flesh out the dream. This may involve learning new skills; it definitely involves discipline and hard work. But if we will believe in our God-given dreams and our abilities to see them through, we will be happier individuals and our world will be a better place.

Lesson 2: We can have spirit-controlled temperaments.

"If I had twelve children, I guess they would all be different," my mother often said as she shook her head in amazement at the differences in her own three. Why should we be surprised that there are such vast differences in one family? We each get a different set of genes. Some of these genes are similar, but some are from grandparents—even great grandparents. I have a nephew, Danny, whose grandfather died before Danny was born. Yet, even without ever knowing him, Danny walks, talks, and gestures like his grandfather. Danny is the only person in his family who received such a complete set of his grandfather's genes.

Add to the gene pool our environment. No two children are reared in exactly the same environment, even if they are part of the same family. Parents are younger when one child is born and older when another is born. Family situations change, such as finances or health, and the number and size of family problems differ. For example, my father went through several years of alcoholism, but it didn't seem to affect my sister or brother in the same way it affected me. My older sister was already out of college and teaching in another town. She knew about his alcoholism only through correspondence and rare visits home. Similarly, my much younger brother was almost unaware of what was happening. I had a sensitive and melancholic temperament and was in the midst of the vulnerable years of high school and college. In addition, I adored my dad, so his alcoholism was traumatic for me.

All children are born with a bent toward certain personality traits, which is considered their temperament. The best-known and most widely accepted basic temperaments were propounded by Hippocrates, the brilliant Greek physician and philosopher, and later popularized by Immanuel Kant. They are:

1. Sanguine: an outgoing, talkative, people-loving individual who is able to enjoy the present and not worry too much about the future. True sanguines awaken humming or singing. If you are married to one and you are not an early morning person, your spouse will drive you crazy. The motto for sanguines is "Don't worry. Be happy."
2. Choleric: a quick-moving, active, independent, strong-willed, decisive, and practical individual; a born leader. The choleric thrive on activity. The motto is: "Let's get on with it."
3. Melancholic: by nature, an introvert who is analytical, sensitive, dependable, self-sacrificing, and moody. Those with a melancholic temperament are often perfectionists. The motto is: "Let's think about this."
4. Phlegmatic: a calm, cool, collected, laid back, and easy going individual who has a wry sense of humor and is sometimes lazy. The motto is: "That's the way the cookie crumbles."

Obviously, one temperament isn't better than another—only different. Also, no one is a pure type. After all, we get our genes from four grandparents as well as our parents. But we are predominantly more one than another. The glorious thing is that when Christ, through the Holy Spirit, lives in us as King, who reigns for a lifetime (rather than as a President, who will be replaced by someone else), we never stay the way we are.

The Holy Spirit comes to us at baptism and becomes more and more dominant within us as we seek to live in daily fellowship with Christ. The presence of the Holy Spirit helps us become more Christlike, so that our rough edges are softened and we are made strong in our broken places. I have observed this transformation in so many Christians. For example, the sanguine individual's random socializing becomes a spiritual gift of hospitality; the hot-tempered choleric individual is softened by patience and understanding; the moody melancholic individual becomes the positive caregiver; and the laid back phlegmatic individual can radiate the joy of the Lord. Thanks be to God: We don't have to stay the way we are! As Mary and Martha discovered, we can have spirit-controlled temperaments!

Digging a Little Deeper

1. Read Luke 10:40-42. Why did Jesus rebuke Martha? What was the source of her distraction and worry? In what way was Martha a perfectionist? What is "the better part" to which Jesus referred? Ask yourself: What is the source of my worry? What is keeping me from finding "the better part"?
2. Read Matthew 6:25-34. Is it ever appropriate or beneficial to worry? What is the difference between worry and concern?
3. In your own words, define or explain the word *faith*. How can feelings sometimes limit our capacity to have faith? How can feelings also be a benefit to our faith? Discuss.
4. Compare the account of Jesus' visit to Mary and Martha's home (Luke 10:38-42) to the account of his encounter with them after Lazarus's death (John 11:17-29). In what way did Jesus help each of the women see the need for personal growth? Discuss.
5. Do you more readily identify with Mary or Martha? Discuss.
6. As a young wife and mother, I completely identified with Martha. I was distracted by many things and naturally felt that Jesus should have sent Mary right out to help Martha. It

didn't take long, however, for me to realize the disastrous results of my parched spirit: not only distractions and worry, but also irritation, impatience, and resentment. What other results of a parched spirit have you experienced in your own life or observed in the lives of others?

7. Jesus wisely knew that our priorities must be in order: "But seek first his kingdom and his righteousness, and all these things will be given to you" (Matthew 6:33 NIV). Look at your own life. Are your priorities in order, or are you "majoring in minors"? Discuss.

8. What is your temperament? Are you more of a left brain thinker, like Martha (practical, no-nonsense person with good organizational skills), or a right brain thinker, like Mary (creative and intuitive yet often fragmented)? How can the balanced presence of Jesus help you to be a whole brain thinker? Discuss.

4.

A Healed Mind

Scripture Text: **Luke 8:1c-2; John 19:25, 20:1-18**

The Twelve were with him, and also some women who had been cured of evil spirits and diseases: Mary (called Magdalene) from whom seven demons had come out.

—*Luke 8:1c-2 NIV*

Early on the first day of the week, while it was still dark, Mary Magdalene went to the tomb and saw that the stone had been removed from the entrance.

—*John 20:1 NIV*

Mary Magdalene's Story

Mary Magdalene walked away from the other believers to be alone and think about the resurrection she had witnessed. As she passed a stream, she caught a glimpse of herself. She was tall, slender, and erect, with auburn hair that cascaded over her shoulders. As so many had told her, she had beauty of face and form. The peaceful poise in her facial expression was far different from the tortured expression she had worn on the first day she had met Jesus. The memory was as fresh as if it had occurred yesterday. She still wept when she thought of it.

Their meeting had happened on a day when Jesus and his disciples had come to the town of Magdala on the northwest shore of the Sea of Galilee. The travelers actually had hoped to rest there; but as usually happened when people heard that Jesus was coming, everyone brought their ill relatives to Jesus for healing. Mary's cousins, who were convinced that she was possessed of seven demons, had brought her screaming, cursing, and kicking into the presence of the Healer.

After the healing, Mary's cousins had told her how she had looked before Jesus' touch changed her—disheveled hair, wild eyes, hunched shoulders, and a look of angry defiance on her face. She could remember how tortured she had felt. She had experienced feelings of fear, distress, and helplessness. Stronger than that memory, though, was the memory of Jesus' touch on her shoulder—and his calm, compassionate voice. At first, she had pulled away in panic; but with his second touch, she had felt a deep peace filling her body and mind. Her mind had become as tranquil as the waters of the Sea of Galilee after Jesus calmed the storm (Mark 4:39). She remembered standing slowly, smoothing her hair, straightening her shoulders, and returning the smile of the man who had made her whole.

For several days afterward, she had been concerned that the healing might not last, that the "episodes"—what we would call mental illness today—might recur. But her healing had lasted all these years, and she had experienced the most glorious period of her life as she had helped Jesus in his ministry.

Then she remembered the torture of her soul—far worse than the earlier torture of her mind—as she had watched the unjust trial and ignominious crucifixion of the most righteous man she had ever known. The crucifixion scene had been so horrible that most of the disciples, including Peter, had deserted Jesus. For her, it had been unthinkable that she would not be with him to the end. Though she had felt helpless to do anything to stop the tragedy, she had wanted to offer her moral and spiritual support (Luke 23:49; John 19:25).

Her recollections led to another memory—one with eternal significance—that she hoped never to lose: It was she who first found the stone rolled away from the tomb (John 20:1-2), and it was she, a woman, to whom the Lord had made his first resurrection appearance (John 20:10-18; Mark 16:9-11).[1]

As she sat by the cypress tree near the stream and remembered, she could still hear the sound of Jesus' voice as he called her by name: "Mary." She no longer felt fear. She knew that eternal life for the believer was assured, just as he had promised: "I am the resurrection and the life. He who believes in me will live, even though he dies; and whoever lives and believes in me will never die" (John 11:25 NIV).

Though Mary Magdalene probably never knew the apostle Paul, at that moment she could have affirmed the words he would speak much later: "If we live, we live to the Lord; and if we die, we die to the Lord. So, whether we live or die, we belong to the Lord" (Romans 14:8 NIV).

What Can We Learn from Mary Magdalene?

Lesson 1: We, too, need to be healed by Jesus.

Like Mary Magdalene, we need to be healed of our "demons." For some of us, these "demons" manifest themselves

---

[1] In the Synoptic Gospels, Mary Magdalene is accompanied by two women: Mary the mother of James the younger and Joses, and Salome, the mother of Zebedee's sons, according to Mark 15:40 and Matthew 27:56; or Mary the mother of James, and Joanna, according to Luke 24:10. John mentions only Mary Magdalene in his Gospel account, but her words to Peter—"They have taken the Lord out of the tomb, and *we* don't know where they have put him!" (John 20:2 NIV, emphasis added)—may indicate that her companions were with her.

in physical ways. Indeed, those who have suffered from an addiction or any form of mental illness may feel at times as though they are possessed by demons.

I know a woman who once suffered from bipolar (manic-depressive) illness. When in the manic stage, she had seemingly endless energy. She could wash cabinets, clean closets, and scrub floors until well past midnight. She literally could "shop until she dropped." In her depressive stage, she would sit motionless in a darkened room or sleep. After her illness was diagnosed, her medications kept her balanced so that she could function normally.

I have another friend who suffered for years from chronic depression. She called it her "journey into nowhere" because of the darkness and despair she felt. She once told me, "I felt as if I were caught in the clutches of a force beyond myself." It took four years of Christian counseling, medication, and a new spiritual experience to restore her to wholeness.

Indeed, God can heal all our physical and mental demons through doctors, medicine, counseling, and new spiritual experiences. One person may need all of these, while another needs only one or two. God tailors the treatment to our individual needs. This help becomes operative only when we recognize our need and are willing to seek help.

For others of us, the demons that torment us are sins of the spirit. In the book *Grace Abounding to the Chief of Sinners* (London: SCM Press, 1955), John Bunyan wrote: "I find to this day these seven abominations in my heart" (p. 148). Pride, envy, anger, intemperance, lasciviousness, covetousness, spiritual sloth—these were also the seven scars on Dante's sanctified head. Therefore it is better to enter into heaven with seven devils excavated out of our hearts as with a knife, than have them gnawing in our hearts through all eternity. Sins of the spirit may not be as readily visible as physical or mental illness, but their results can be even more devastating.

From my own experience battling pride, jealousy, and many years, I know that sins of the spirit bring much fragmentation and no inner peace. In retrospect, I realize that my pride stems in part from insecurity and the need for recognition and approval. Likewise, jealousy is always the backwash of insecurity. As for my anger, I didn't begin to discover its source until one day when I saw the look of pain in the eyes of my seven-year-old son when I spoke to him in anger. That day, as I realized the effect my anger had on my young son, I made the decision to search for the source of my anger and, with God's help, to overcome it. It took several years of reading everything I could find on the subject, especially books by Christian psychiatrists. I discovered that my anger likely had begun when my father was an alcoholic. I had not wanted to face my anger then, so I had pushed it down into my subconscious mind where it had festered, popping up at the most unexpected times. Also, I learned that a parent's unjustified anger can create false guilt in a child.

My desire for wholeness became greater than my need to be a perfectionist or to get my own way. Overcoming my anger involved several stages: recognizing my needs, repenting, seeking and receiving God's forgiveness, and growing in my understanding of myself as a person of worth—created by God, redeemed by Christ, and empowered by the Holy Spirit. Perhaps most important, I learned to have a more disciplined prayer life in which I could experience the touch of Jesus on my life.

For most of us, the demons we experience from time to time are simply feelings of fatigue, meaninglessness, or *ennui* ("What's the use?"). When I feel empty or parched in my spirit, I use this formula:

1. Get plenty of sleep
2. Exercise (out of doors, if possible)
3. "Rest in the Lord" (Isaiah 40:31)

4. Read God's Word (John 15 always speaks to my spirit.)
5. Talk to a trusted friend
6. Give thanks for your blessings (This opens our hearts to God and life.)
7. Wait for God's healing touch

Sometimes this process takes several days, but it never fails to get my spirit singing.

If we are to grow more and more into the likeness of Christ, we often will need, as did Mary Magdalene, a touch from Jesus. The words of one popular hymn describe the feeling that comes from discovering the presence of Jesus in our lives, as he frees us from the worry and the burdens that have held us captive in the past:

> Then the hand of Jesus touched me,
> and now I am no longer the same.
> (William J. Gaither, "He Touched Me," 1963)

Remember that living in an imperfect world where there is pain, sorrow, and evil does not encourage personal wholeness. Add to that our own bad choices and life circumstances, and we all need many touches from Christ.

Lesson 2: It is easy to misrepresent others, just as Mary Magdalene often is misrepresented.

Where did we get the idea that Mary Magdalene was a prostitute? The Bible doesn't say that. It says that she was a woman "from whom seven demons had come out" (Luke 8:2 NIV). Yet many artists and playwrights have portrayed her as a courtesan or a profligate woman. Many houses for "fallen women" have been called "Magdalene Houses."

In the movie *The Robe* (1953), which is based on a novel by the same name written by Lloyd C. Douglas, there is a scene that, although dramatically impressive, suggests Mary

Magdalene's past was not too virtuous. Mary Magdalene and Mary, the mother of Jesus, are trying to get close to the cross at the time of the crucifixion. A Roman guard is restraining them. Suddenly Mary Magdalene reaches up to remove a comb, which allows her hair to cascade below her shoulders. Then she says rather seductively, "Marcellus." After turning around, the guard takes a second look at her and exclaims, "Mary! I didn't recognize you. You have changed." Mary points toward the cross and replies with deep feeling, "Yes, Marcellus, I've changed. He changed me."

Through the years, I even have heard ministers speak of Mary Magdalene as the sinful woman who entered the house of the Pharisee. She wet Jesus' feet with her tears, kissed them, and wiped them with her hair before she poured perfume on them (Luke 7:36-38). Mary Magdalene may have been that woman, but there is no shred of evidence in the Bible to prove it.

In the book *All the Women of the Bible*, Herbert Lockyer explains that these beliefs about Mary Magdalene stem from a legend in the Jewish *Talmud* that says Mary had an unsavory reputation (Grand Rapids: Zondervan, 1967, p. 100). That legend, along with the fact that Luke places the first reference to Mary Magdalene (Luke 8:2) just after the story of the sinful woman (Luke 7:36-50), has caused many people to believe that she was a prostitute. But there is no genuine evidence of this.

How easily we misrepresent others. Sometimes it happens when we pass on something we've heard about someone. Sometimes it happens when we describe someone after a first encounter that didn't give us an adequate picture of the whole person. Other times, despite our best intentions, we simply get the facts wrong.

I have to laugh about an erroneous description given of my husband and me to one of the first churches he served as pastor.

It was not a harmful description, just an incorrect one. This was the description: "The new pastor is tall, dignified, and never smiles. His wife is short, fat, and jolly." It is true that Ralph is tall and has a sense of presence in the pulpit, but he is humorous and playful and thoroughly enjoys life. I am indeed short (five feet three inches), but I have always been a size 4 or 6. And though I don't think of myself as "jolly," I love to laugh and have a positive sense of joy. Needless to say, everyone who had heard the description was surprised when they met us. It turned out that the man who started the rumor had been given the descriptions of two ministerial couples—one going to a nearby church, and us. He simply got them mixed up.

We must be careful not to pass on a rumor without checking the facts. Even then, if something we hear is harmful, we should not pass it on. Harmful rumors can ruin reputations, careers, and lives. It is always important for us to speak truthfully; and as Christians, we need to speak the truth in kindness with respect for the person about whom we speak. This belief is emphasized throughout the book of Proverbs. I especially like Proverbs 31:26, which says, "She opens her mouth with wisdom, and on her tongue is the law of kindness" (NKJV). One of the verses in the New Testament that speaks clearly of this belief is Ephesians 4:15: "Instead, speaking the truth in love, we will in all things grow up into him who is the Head, that is, Christ" (NIV). Similarly, in James 3:1-9 we learn the power of the tongue for good or evil and how to tame the tongue to bring it under the Lordship of Christ.

Perhaps our motto as Christians should be Ephesians 4:29: "Do not let any unwholesome talk come out of your mouths, but only what is helpful for building others up according to their needs, that it may benefit those who listen" (NIV). If we observe this motto, then we will never misrepresent others in our conversations!

Lesson 3: Like Mary Magdalene at the tomb, we sometimes seek the wrong form of Jesus.

Mary Magdalene was looking for a dead Christ. She said to the gardener: "Sir, if you have carried him away, tell me where you have put him, and I will get him" (John 20:15 NIV). Some people think Jesus was a wonderful man who did great things during his lifetime on Earth. Some even see him as the Son of God who was sent to Earth to show us how to live. But they do not see him as the living Christ who, through the Holy Spirit, can live in us today.

It was William Law, the eighteenth-century Christian mystic and author from King's Cliffe, England, who said: "A Christ not in us is the same thing as a Christ not ours" (*The Spirit of Prayer*, 1749). It is a daily relationship with this Christ that empowers and guides our living. When we invite Christ into our lives, we accept a partnership. It helps me to remember that I am working in tandem with him. I ask each morning: "Well, what are *we* going to do today?" Asking that simple question, plus freely talking with him throughout the day, changes my perspective on the circumstances and persons I encounter. Many young Christians today wear bracelets with the initials WWJD—"What Would Jesus Do?" This reminds them that they are alive in Christ. His spirit within empowers and directs their lives. Regardless of the "method" we use, each of us must find a way to remind ourselves of the constancy of our relationship with Christ.

Words from the Easter hymn "He Lives" have always reminded me that Christ's resurrection transformed a band of dispirited disciples into a radiant band with courage to dare anything and do it: "I serve a risen savior. He's in the world today" (Alfred H. Ackley, The Rodeheaver Co., 1933). Through committed disciples who were "alive in Christ," the Christian church, despite persecution and enormous difficulties, has brought the good news of the gospel to nearly every part of the world and has changed the face of humanity. The power of this gospel is ours if we seek and serve not a dead man who was a good example but a living Savior who "is in the world today."

Lesson 4: We should follow Jesus out of gratitude for the healing and wholeness we receive from him.

Mary Magdalene certainly followed Jesus out of gratitude. That wasn't true of all the people Jesus healed. In Luke 17:11-19, there is a wonderful story about Jesus entering a "certain village" (v. 12 KJV). Traveling on the border from Galilee to Samaria, Jesus was on his final journey to Jerusalem. There were ten lepers in that village who called out to him simultaneously: "Jesus, Master, have pity on us!" (v. 13 NIV). In that day, lepers were required by law to stay a safe distance from others and to call out in a loud voice if others came too close.

Even knowing that he was facing a cross in Jerusalem, Jesus had compassion on the ten lepers, one of whom was a Samaritan. Ordinarily, Jews would never have associated with the Samaritans, whom they considered to be half-breeds. Isn't it interesting that racial and creedal prejudices are forgotten in a common disaster? We seem to learn in pain what we refuse to learn in joy.

Because leprosy sometimes went into remission, a leper who believed that his disease had gone away was to present himself to the priest, who would declare him clean (Leviticus 14). Jesus was asking the lepers to act in faith and go to the priest, even though at the moment they were not free of the disease. Perhaps all they needed was a bit of hope. And they acted upon his command. On the way to the priest, Jesus healed the lepers; but only one of the ten returned to thank Jesus. Why? My guess is that they went straight home to their families and neighbors to display the miracle. That seems logical, for most people would want to do this after a lengthy illness and absence from home.

Why, then, did Jesus make it an issue? Jesus asked, "Were not all ten cleansed? Where are the other nine? Was no one found to return and give praise to God except this foreigner?" (Luke 17:17-18 NIV). I certainly don't believe Jesus raised the issue because his feelings were hurt or because he wanted to teach social graces to the lepers. Rather, he was emphasizing the importance of expressing gratitude to God. Ingratitude snaps our hearts shut, but gratitude opens them to God, to others, and to life. I am convinced that gratitude may be the greatest of all virtues, for out of it flow humility, peace, contentment, motivation, and joy.

Gratitude changed my life. It allowed me to see life as an incredible gift—as a privilege, not a right. It enabled me never to take people or circumstances for granted. I learned its power following the death of our older son, Rick, who was critically injured in an accident and died ten days later. He had just turned twenty and was a student at a local university. It was such a traumatic experience that I had a very difficult time overcoming my grief. Each night when I went to bed, I felt as if there were black clouds hanging over my head. When I awakened the following morning, the clouds were still there. Although I never once blamed God for the accident and prayed regularly, I still was having problems handling my grief. I learned that something of yourself dies when one of your children dies.

One comfort during this time was to reread Paul's words to the Thessalonians: "Give thanks in all circumstances, for this is God's will for you in Christ Jesus" (1 Thessalonians 5:18 NIV). Paul did not say we are to give thanks *for* all circumstances. He didn't suggest that I give thanks that my son had died; rather, his words meant that in the midst of tragedy, I should give thanks.

That simple statement transformed my perspective. Each morning before I got out of bed to exercise, I conditioned my mind with gratitude. Instead of focusing on what I had lost, I focused on what I still had. For example, upon awakening I would say something like this: "Thank you, God, for your love made evident in Jesus Christ. Thank you for a husband who loves me. Thank you that we have another son. Thank you that we had Rick for twenty years—and for our happy memories. Thank you for friends, for a job to occupy my mind during much of each day, and for the church that is truly the body of Christ." Each day I could feel my grief lifting. That morning exercise of gratitude was so life-changing that I continue it to this day. On the rare occasions when I oversleep and don't take time to count my blessings, I am irritable and impatient with others.

My observation is that grateful people express their thanks in acts of appreciation. Small expressions of appreciation—even as small as a thank-you note—can enrich and change the climate of a marriage, a friendship, a parent-child relationship, or any organization. By the same token, ingratitude can break a company, a marriage, a church, an office, or a friendship.

Even more important, ingratitude can destroy our relationship with God. We can block our "pipeline" to God with ingratitude, anxiety, and other negative emotions. Let us remember that the attitude of gratitude keeps our hearts open to God's love, creative ideas, peace, and power.

Digging a Little Deeper

1. There are four kinds of healing: physical, mental, emotional, and spiritual. Jesus helped persons in each of these areas. What two kinds of healing did Jesus bring Mary Magdalene? (See Luke 8:2.) Which kind(s) of healing do you most need in your life? What steps do you need to take to seek healing and wholeness? Discuss.
2. On days when you are feeling down, dispirited, or draggy,

what do you do to enable your spirit to "sing" again? Reread the formula in Lesson 1. Which of these suggestions is or could be most helpful to you? Why?

3. In many books and movies, Mary Magdalene is portrayed as a prostitute before meeting Jesus, despite the fact that there is no biblical evidence of this. Why is she portrayed this way? Have you ever passed on a rumor about someone and later found it to be false? How did you feel? What did you do? As Christians, what should we do to prevent hurting others in this way? Discuss.

4. What are some different views people have about who Jesus was/is? Read Philippians 1:21, Romans 14:8, and Galatians 2:20. What does the apostle Paul tell us in these verses about "the living Christ"? How does Christ live in us? Describe or tell what it means to have Christ living in you.

5. Read Luke 17:11-19, the story of Jesus and the ten lepers. Why do you think only one leper returned to thank Jesus? What lesson can we learn from this story? Why is gratitude necessary for abundant living?

6. Ask yourself, "Have I said 'thank you' today—not only to God, but also to those around me: family, friends, colleagues, neighbors?" What are some ways we can express gratitude to others? Discuss.

For the Journey Ahead

1. Memorize the following biblical affirmations and repeat them on down days:

   • They that wait upon the LORD shall renew their strength; they shall mount up with wings as eagles; they shall run, and not be weary; and they shall walk, and not faint. (Isaiah 40:31 KJV)

- If God be for us [me], who can be against us [me]? (Romans 8:31 KJV)
- He who has begun a good work in you will complete it. (Philippians 1:6 NKJV)
- I can do all things through Christ who strengthens me. (Philippians 4:13 NKJV)
- "These things have I spoken unto you, that my joy might remain in you, and that your joy might be full." (John 15:11 KJV)
- "With God all things are possible." (Matthew 19:26 KJV)
- "Lo, I am with you always, even to the end of the age." (Matthew 28:20 NKJV)

2. Cultivate an attitude of gratitude. Here are a few disciplines to help you. If you follow these disciplines, your heart will be flooded with joy and humility.

- For one month, pray by saying only "thank you." Do not ask for anything. In the words of an old hymn: "Count your blessings, name them one by one, and it will surprise you what the Lord has done" ("Count Your Blessings," Johnson Oatman Jr. and Edwin O. Excell, 1897).
- For one week, look for as many people as possible to whom you can express genuine appreciation—a teenager who makes a bed, a spouse who does something kind for you, a speaker, a teacher, a minister, a friend, or even a stranger. (Once I was fumbling in my purse for change to put into the parking meter. Suddenly a stranger walked by and dropped a quarter in the meter for me. "Wait," I said, "how will I repay you?" Continuing to walk, he called out, "Just pass it on.")
- Think of some people who have influenced your life for good. If they are living, write them a note. If they are not living, give thanks to God for their influence.

5.

Mary,
the Mother of Mark

She Helped Build Up
the Body of Christ

Scripture Text: **Acts 12:12-13**

He [Peter] went to the house of Mary the mother of John, also called Mark, where many people had gathered and were praying. Peter knocked at the outer entrance, and a servant girl named Rhoda came to answer the door.

—Acts 12:12-13 NIV

Mary's Story

It was early in the new year, but the weather was unseasonably warm for Jerusalem. Mary was returning to her home after delivering food to a widow who was ill. The woman was only one of several new Christians for whom Mary had accepted personal responsibility.

I wonder where Paul, Barnabas, and John Mark are right now, she thought as she stopped to observe some new buds on a dogwood tree. *Wherever they are, I hope that the weather there is as nice as it is here. How exciting to think that this new faith could reach beyond Jerusalem and surrounding areas to Asia Minor—and maybe even to Europe!* Realistically, Mary knew that this would be an arduous, even dangerous journey. She, along with the other Jerusalem Christians, prayed daily for the apostles. She prayed that each of the men would be given special strength, patience, and joy for the journey. She especially prayed for her young son, John Mark. After all, he was only twenty years old; and due to his father's business success, Mark had never suffered real hardship. Mary's wise husband had provided so well for his family financially that even after his death, they had no sense of deprivation.

How I miss him, she thought as she meandered slowly through the winding streets. *I wish Mark had the benefit of his father's wisdom. Oh, Mark is a diligent worker in the family business and an eager new Christian who was thrilled to be invited to go on the first missionary journey. I'm sure that it was my nephew Barnabas who persuaded Paul to allow such a young man to accompany them.*

By the time she reached her home, which was located on the south end of the western hill of Mt. Zion, she could look down on her beloved city of Jerusalem. Since the elevation was so much greater on Mt. Zion than in the city, it was at least ten degrees cooler. On summer evenings, it was pleasant to sit in her courtyard, look down on the lights, and hear the sounds of the ancient city.

When Mary entered her commodious home, she was amazed to see all the servants vigorously cleaning the house—something she had not requested.

"What's happening here? Are we having unexpected company?"

Benjamin, the majordomo replied, "Since it is so warm, we decided to get a head start on spring cleaning." With her eyes dancing, Rhoda, the youngest and most exuberant servant, who recently had become a Christian, blurted out, "Besides, we know a secret!" She was reprimanded by the tone in Benjamin's voice as he said sharply, "Rhoda!"

"Benjamin, why don't you follow me into the library," Mary called out as she walked briskly through the elegantly furnished living room. "Close the door, please," she said to Benjamin when he entered the comfortable room. "What is going on out there, and what is the secret?"

"Well, m'am, your sister, the mother of Barnabas, sent a messenger to say that John Mark would be coming home—probably arriving tonight. It was to be a surprise, and we knew that you would like the house to be clean and look its best."

"Mark's coming home tonight?" Mary exclaimed excitedly. "I can't wait to see him!" Then, as an afterthought, she asked, "Are Paul and Barnabas returning also?"

"The messenger only said Mark, m'am, so I'm not sure about the other two."

After dismissing Benjamin, Mary flew into action. She inspected every corner of her son's room—and even turned down his bed. Rhoda served Mary dinner in her bedroom. Since Mark wasn't home yet, Mary knew that it might be late before he arrived. She wanted to be rested so that she and her son could talk about his experiences.

"Isn't it exciting that John Mark is coming home," said Rhoda as she danced all around the room. "Benjamin didn't want me to say anything, but I just couldn't keep quiet."

"Don't worry, Rhoda," replied Mary as she patted the girl's shoulder. "This way I can be more prepared to see him."

"Thank you. If you need anything else, m'am, you just call me," she said as she fairly floated out of the room.

As Mary finished her dinner, a disturbing thought suddenly came to her: *Why was Mark coming home? Was he ill? Had he been in an accident? They had planned to be away much longer. Were the others coming with Mark?* The thoughts kept her from the sleep she had planned. Then, at almost midnight, she heard his steps in the courtyard. She would know those steps anywhere. They were firm and fast. She ran to the door and took him into her arms. They clung to each other a long moment before Mary held him at arm's length and said, "Here. Let me look at you." Looking intently in her son's face, she declared, "You are much too thin. Didn't they give you anything to eat?"

Pulling away, Mark paced back and forth in the room, saying nervously, "Oh, yes, I had plenty to eat. It wasn't the food."

"Then what?" asked Mary. "Something is wrong. We have always been honest with each other, so tell me what it is." Sensing her son's fatigue, she added, "Mark, would you rather talk about it after you have had a good night's sleep?"

"No," he replied emphatically—and with some irritation. "I want to talk about it now and be done with it." He hesitated for a moment while pacing the floor. Then he blurted out, "I'm just so frustrated with Brother Paul! He treated us all like servants—'Go do this, go do that.' He pushed us unmercifully. Oh, I know you think he is this great Christian, and I suppose he is, but I just couldn't take all those horrible conditions. I missed having my own bed and decent food to eat."

As she tried to size up the situation, Mary asked, "Did they still need you when you left?"

"Oh, yes," the young man said almost sarcastically. "I was Brother Paul's personal attendant, which means his chief servant." Almost to herself, Mary said, "I wonder if your father and I have made life too easy for you."

"I knew you would blame me, and it is not my fault!" But his voice quivered, and Mary saw tears in his eyes. She reached out her hand to him as she had done so often when he was a child, and he buried his head in her lap.

"Oh, Mother, I'm so ashamed. I was honored when Barnabas invited me to go on the first missionary journey, but I failed, Mother. I was so homesick. I hope God will forgive me."

"He already has, Son, and so do I."

"I want to serve Christ, and I will; but I need to grow up. Please help me."

"I will, Mark. And you will have other great opportunities."

———————

Obviously, the preceding scene is imaginary, but something like this could have happened. What we do know is that John Mark did grow up. He accompanied Barnabas on another missionary journey (Acts 15:36-41), and he wrote one of the most succinct and straightforward accounts of the life of Christ (the Gospel of Mark). Mark was so involved in the life of the early church that Peter referred affectionately to him as "Mark my son" (1 Peter 5:13 NKJV). We also know that Mark was with Paul during his imprisonment in Rome (2 Timothy 4:11). Mark not only grew up; he became a mature Christian who was effective in the extension of the faith. Tradition tells us that Mark founded the church in the Jewish-Greek city of Alexandria (Edith Deen, *All of the Women of the Bible*, New York: Harper and Bros. Publishers, 1955, p. 212).

Could Mark have been such a powerful influence in the early church if his mother had not been such a role model of Christian faith, stability, and wisdom? I don't think so! In fact, I never have read the Gospel of Mark without giving thanks for his mother, Mary of Jerusalem.

What Can We Learn from Mary, the Mother of Mark?

Lesson 1: We can serve Christ and his church with our spiritual gifts.

Mary had the spiritual gifts of hospitality and generosity (giving), and she used them for the benefit of the early church.

Though there is little information about Mary in scripture (Acts 12:12), many scholars believe that it was her home where Jesus had the last supper with his disciples (William Barclay, *The Acts of the Apostles,* Philadelphia: Westminster Press, 1955, p. 101) and where Christian disciples gathered at the time of Pentecost (Deen, *All of the Women of the Bible,* p. 212). We can imagine Mary's home was spacious enough for such accommodations, for it appears that Rhoda was only one of the maids in Mary's home (Acts 12:13). We also know that it was Mary's home where Peter returned to join his fellow Christians after his escape from prison (Acts 12:5-19). Because Herod was persecuting Christians at the time, it took great courage and devotion to her faith for Mary to open her home for prayer and worship. Yet she used her gifts freely.

When I began to study Mary, the mother of John Mark, I thought immediately of my late friend Georgianna Webb, who lost her battle against lung cancer when she was fifty-eight. I first met Georgianna soon after she and her husband, Ray, were married and they joined our church. At the time, it was my privilege to organize a new Sunday school class for young adults, and both of them were valuable members. Immediately I recognized that Georgianna had two talents that were vital in growing a class: hospitality and organizational skills. She was generous in using both of these to build up the class.

Georgianna's hospitable personality made everyone feel welcome. After arriving at class early each Sunday, she would greet each person and help him or her feel comfortable and meet others in the class. One shy young woman once told me, "When I am around Georgianna, I feel that God has just reached out and put his arms around me." What a ministry!

Georgianna also used her organizational skills to put together a church cookbook to raise money for a mission project sponsored by our class. It was an awesome task. She saw the project through every step, from collecting recipes to printing, marketing, and selling copies. The book ran into several printings, and now, twenty-five years later, it has become the "kitchen Bible" to women of the church.

As a result of the talents of many individuals, the class grew quite large, and we developed several small study and share groups. The purpose of these groups was to enable members to know one another better and to enhance their spiritual growth. Some groups were for couples and some were for stay-at-home moms. In one of these groups, Georgianna came to a new commitment to Christ and a deep desire to serve others in his name. Her talents of hospitality and organization then became her spiritual gifts through which she blessed every life she touched.

Our special spiritual gifts may not be hospitality or generosity (giving) or organization (administration), yet like my friend, Georgianna, and Mary, the mother of Mark, we can work to develop these qualities and use the unique gifts we have been given to help others and thus build up the body of Christ.

Lesson 2: We should encourage those we love, especially our children, to serve Christ and his church.

Mary was supportive, not possessive, of her only child. There is no indication in scripture that Mark went on the first missionary journey in order to get away from home. Indeed, since most scholars believe that Mark left the missionary journey because of homesickness, as well as the rigors of the journey, we can assume there was a close relationship between mother and son. Also, because Mark later did so many things for the expansion of the Christian church, it is obvious that Mary was not possessive but supportive of her son's ministry.

It is easy for us, as women, to be possessive of the people we love, especially our children. In some ways, they seem to be extensions of ourselves. I can imagine what a temptation it would be to be possessive if you had lost your husband and had only one child. Perhaps we ought to remember two quotations. The first comes from Kahlil Gibran's book *The Prophet*: "Your children . . . come through you . . . yet they belong not to you" (New York: Alfred A. Knopf, 1923). The second is Jewell Bothwell Tull in the poem "Coquette" where she writes that we should lightly hold those we love, for

> Things with wings held tightly,
> Want to go.
> (in Burton Stevenson's *The Home Book of Quotations*,
> New York: Dodd, Mead & Company, 1967)

I admire tremendously this Mary of Jerusalem. Her hospitality and generosity of spirit not only helped the early church grow but also blessed so many people in the process. It's evident that she had the same generosity of possessions, for as we've seen, she freely opened her home as a place of worship and prayer. But for even more than these qualities, I admire her for passing on the Christian faith to her son and then allowing him to make mistakes on his way to becoming a self-reliant man and a strong, independent Christian leader. My guess is that it would have been easier for her to keep him tied to the "family business," justifying this by saying he was needed to help keep the family home open to the emerging church. Evidently, she did not do this but, instead, encouraged him to make a strong contribution for Christ.

We can encourage those we love—especially our children and grandchildren—to make a strong contribution for Christ by being happy, radiant role models. If on rare occasions I don't feel excited about going to Sunday school and worship, I think of my diminutive but vivacious grandmother. I have a special memory of an overnight visit to her home when she fairly sang these words as she gave me a bath: "Tomorrow is Sunday, and we are going to Sunday school and church!" She said the words with excitement and anticipation. After all these years, I have a sense of expectation as I head toward church on Sunday morning. My grandmother was also a role model of service to Christ in the church and community.

When I asked my husband if his parents encouraged him to become an ordained minister, he said, "Not once." It was only after he felt called into the ministry and began his theological training that his mother said, "I always prayed that one of our four sons would go into the ministry." It was his parents' happy and faithful following of Christ that most influenced their son.

Let's remember, too, that other children and youth in our churches and neighborhoods are watching to see if we are "for real." So we should not discuss church problems in their presence. Whether we're being watched by family, friends, or complete strangers, let's always be sure that our strong morality is tempered with joy and kindness so that we can say with Nehemiah: "The joy of the Lord is your [my] strength" (Nehemiah 8:10).

Lesson 3: Prayer gives us the courage and strength we need to serve God.

Mary had the courage to live out her Christian convictions, which was not an easy thing to do in her day. Herod Agrippa was in power, and he had curried favor with the Jews by observing their feast days and their rules. In all likelihood, it was the Jews' dislike of the new Christian sect that prompted Herod to persecute them (Acts 12:1-11). James, the brother of John the sons of Zebedee, had been killed; and Peter was in prison. According to Jewish law, Peter could not be executed during the Feast of the Passover. On the night before the Feast ended, Peter miraculously escaped and made his way to the home of Mary, where Christians were praying for his escape (Acts 12:1-19).

Since it was common knowledge that members of the new sect

met in the home of Mary, she, too, was in mortal danger. Yet there is no evidence that she wavered in her faith. She was a steadfast believer, regardless of the circumstances. Evidently, one of the reasons for her faithfulness was her firm belief in the power of prayer. At least in my life, I have discovered that my faithfulness as a disciple is stronger when my prayer life is vital.

For many years, I had a hard time understanding prayer's power. Part of the reason was that, by temperament, I am an activist, not a mystic. There was a twofold explanation for this. During those years, I didn't know anyone who spoke of a power-ful prayer life, and I was busy doing what I thought should be done. Also, my education had emphasized the power of science to bring about results. Yet when I looked at all the great Christians I knew or knew of, I saw that each had a disciplined prayer life. Among them was Martin Luther, who reportedly said that he would rather have an army against him than a hundred men and women praying (*The Interpreter's Bible,* vol. 9, Nashville: Abingdon-Cokesbury Press, 1954, p. 157). Others included John Wesley, the father of Methodism; Susanna Wesley, his mother; Charles Spurgeon, renowned theologian and preacher; E. Stanley Jones, missionary to India and evangelist to America; the great Japanese Christian Toyohiko Kagawa; and more contemporary Christians such as Harry Emerson Fosdick, Corrie Ten Boom, Elizabeth Elliot, and hundreds of others. The personal testimonies and life stories of these Christians of power and influence con-vinced me that prayer is truly the source of unbelievable power.

Through the years, I have come to know this incredible power firsthand. A more disciplined prayer life has given me the courage to face life's difficulties, a calmer spirit for everyday liv-ing, and a love for people I don't like. Today, I am certain that prayer is not our moving the arm of God to do what we want. Rather, it is the willingness on our part to be moved by the arm of God to fulfill his purposes in this world. Regrettably, the distractions of our hectic lifestyles keep most of us from the powerful resources that could be ours in prayer.

It seems inevitable that living in this new millennium means living in the "fast lane." Yet in the midst of a technological society and noise pollution, we can have a calm, focused center when we regularly are in the presence of the One who is "the same yesterday and today and forever" (Hebrews 13:8 NIV). Like Mary of Jerusalem, we can make a difference for Christ in our time.

Digging a Little Deeper

1. Read the one scripture verse that tells us about Mary, the mother of John Mark (Acts 12:12). What leads us to believe she had the gifts of hospitality and generosity?
2. Even if hospitality and generosity are not our spiritual gifts, how can we cultivate these qualities in ourselves? Why is it important for all Christians to have these qualities? Discuss.
3. What "clues" can you find in Acts 12:12 13 indicating that Mary was a woman of means with a rather spacious home? Do you think she could have used her gifts of hospitality and generosity as effectively if she had not had these resources? Why or why not? What are some ways we can be hospitable and generous despite humble circumstances or a lack of material possessions?
4. Read Acts 13:13. The Bible does not say why John Mark left the first missionary journey. Some people think that Mark was upset because Barnabas was supposed to be leader of the journey (Acts 13:2) but soon people were talking about "*Paul* and Barnabas" or "*Paul* and his friends" (Acts 13:13). Some say the trip was too hard for him. Some say he was homesick and missed his mother. What do *you* think? Why?
5. Read Acts 12:1-11. It took courage to live as a Christian in a

time of persecution. In what ways today do we need courage in order to live as Christians? In what specific ways do *you* need courage in order to live the Christian life? Discuss.

6. Do you ever find it tempting to hold your loved ones too tightly? Give examples. Why or how do you think that Mary was able to release Mark to greatness?

7. Mary's steadfastness as a Christian evidently came from her devotion to Christ and her prayer life. What do you think would help you to be a more steadfast Christian? Discuss.

8. Knowing that the only thing the disciples asked Jesus to teach them was how to pray (Luke 11:1), we understand something of the power of his prayer life. Think of a person you know who seems to have "prayer power." What are the evidences? Discuss.

9. Have you tapped into the source of power through prayer? If so, give an example of the evidence from your own life—such as the ability to overcome difficulties, courage to take on an awesome responsibility, willingness to "keep on keeping on" in a hard situation, and so forth. If not, why haven't you tapped into the power source? Discuss.

6.

The Woman
with the Issue of Blood

She Had Bedrock Faith

Scripture Text: **Luke 8:43-47**

Now a woman, having a flow of blood for twelve years, who had spent all her livelihood on physicians and could not be healed by any, came from behind and touched the border of His garment. And immediately her flow of blood stopped.

—*Luke 8:43-44 NKJV*

Her Story

Note: Though the following story is mostly imaginary, we know that the woman with the issue of blood was actually healed (Luke 8:43-47) and that the Levitical law (Leviticus 15:19-28) was strictly observed. Although the woman is unnamed in the scripture, Herbert Lockyer notes that the early church is reported to have called her Veronica (All the Women of the Bible, Grand Rapids: Zondervan, 1967, p. 221). As Lockyer also conveys, legend says that she followed Jesus to the cross and that she was the woman who, on the Via Dolorosa, offered him her handkerchief to wipe his face. According to the legend, when Jesus returned the handkerchief, the imprint of his face was upon it. Face cloths from the catacombs of Rome that were alleged to hold the impress of Christ's features were called "Veronicas" (p. 222).

Eusebius the great historian (A.D. 300) says that the woman erected, in her native city, at her own cost, two statues: one of a woman kneeling in suffering and the other of Jesus reaching out his hand to help. It is said that the statues remained until Julian became the Roman Emperor. Julian, wishing to bring back pagan gods, tore down the woman's statues and built his own, which shortly there-after was blasted by a thunderbolt (William Barclay, The Gospel of Luke, *Philadelphia: Westminster Press, 1956, p. 113).*

Regardless of the accuracy of these details, the fact remains that the woman with the issue of blood is a lasting testimony to the power of faith.

Veronica sat listlessly in her bedroom in Caesarea Philippi. Outside, the sky was as blue as an infant's eyes, and the air was delightfully crisp. But in her mind there was only black despair. There seemed to be no hope. Since the birth and death of their only child twelve years ago, she had had uterine hemorrhaging. She and her husband had spent their life savings on every physician who offered her hope—yet to no avail.

The worst part was that according to the Levitical law (Leviticus 15:19-28), she was considered unclean. Anyone who touched her or anything she sat on or lay upon would be unclean. Hence, she couldn't attend the Temple, go to social functions, or have her husband even put his arms around her. This would be bad enough if it were only for seven days—the designated time for the menstrual period—but this had gone on for twelve years. She was physically weak, emaciated, unable to stand for any period of time, and lonely to the core.

Most husbands would have divorced their wives for much less than this, but her husband had been kind. He had sought the help of every physician who thought he could help her; each one had used a high-priced astringent and had spoken magic words. She even had tried home remedies suggested by other women, such as carrying the ashes of an ostrich egg tied in a linen rag in summer and in a cotton rag in winter. Nothing had helped, and all their money was gone. Besides, they knew of no other doctors.

Her husband seemed as dispirited as she was. She suspected now that he was occasionally visiting a prostitute. Why shouldn't he? According to Levitical law, she could not be a wife to him. She wanted to die!

Perhaps if I stop eating completely, she thought to herself, *the end could be near.*

At that moment, there was a loud pounding on her front door and a voice calling, "Veronica, open the door! I found the one who can heal you. Hurry! Hurry!"

It had to be Bernice, the only friend who had dared disobey the law and come to visit. Perhaps by breaking the cycle of isolation, Bernice had preserved Veronica's sanity. In their talking and laughing, Veronica could almost believe that she was normal.

As quickly as her weakness would allow, Veronica walked the length of the house and opened the door.

"Come on! We have to go quickly!" said Bernice. "He is here in our town."

"Wait. Who is this man, and what makes you think he can heal me if all the physicians could not?" Veronica asked.

Bernice slowed her conversation in an effort to explain. "His name is Jesus. He is a traveling teacher and believed by some to be the Messiah. He has healed people of all kinds of illnesses and infirmities, including leprosy, blindness, and paralysis. I've heard that he even enabled one man to rise from the grave, which he had been in for four days."

"Why haven't you told me about him before?" asked Veronica somewhat skeptically.

"Because I didn't think we would ever see him. But he is here in our town now. We must go quickly!"

Suddenly, Veronica's hope—even faith—began to rise like a Phoenix from the ashes. Pulling a shawl around her shoulders, she began to walk quickly—almost running—to keep up with her friend. Then she saw a multitude of people surrounding a very tall man as he sought to move forward. She realized that most of these people knew her to be unclean, and she simply didn't have the courage to push through the crowd to speak to Jesus. She couldn't stand another humiliation.

Yet something stronger than fear seemed to be saying within her, "Touch him. Touch his garment." Though she could see only the back of his head, she pushed close enough to touch one of the tassels on his robe. That touch was like an electric shock going through her body. The hemorrhaging stopped immediately (Luke 8:44). She actually could feel strength returning to her body and color to her cheeks.

Jesus stopped and asked, "Who touched me?"

Peter mildly rebuked him, saying, "Master, the people are crowding and pressing against you."

But Jesus said, "Someone touched me: I know that power has gone out from me."

Then Veronica, realizing that she could not go unnoticed, came forward, fell at Jesus' feet, and told why she had touched him and how she had been healed.

Jesus, using a term of respect and endearment, said, "Daughter, your faith has healed you. Go in peace" (Luke 8:45-48 NIV).

After thanking Jesus and hugging Bernice, Veronica ran like the wind to get home so that she could take a warm bath and put on her prettiest dress. In the meantime, someone who had been with Jesus went to the husband of Veronica and said, "You'd better get home. Something has happened to your wife." Not waiting for more explanation, her husband raced to his home, thinking that his wife had died.

As he opened the front door, he couldn't believe his eyes. Standing before him was the woman he had married fourteen years earlier.

"Veronica, you look beautiful—and so young. Tell me what happened."

With dancing eyes and an energetic voice, she related the entire experience, ending with these words: "I am healed! Jesus made me whole!" Forgetting that the law required them to wait seven days after a cleansing, her husband took Veronica in his arms as his wife.

What Can We Learn from the Woman with the Issue of Blood?

Lesson 1: When we "touch" Christ in faith, we, too, can become whole.

Of all the unnamed women of the Bible, I have a special appreciation for the woman with the issue of blood because she represents a spiritual experience in my own life. For five years before my marriage to a young minister, I had been a director of Christian education and then a conference director of youth ministries. I loved my jobs and thoroughly enjoyed my contact with people, as well as the many affirmations I received. In addition, I had friends and family nearby, a good salary, secretarial help, and freedom to travel. I felt happy and fulfilled.

I knew that after I married the man I loved, I would be moving far away from family and friends and giving up my job (most ministers' wives at that time didn't work outside the home unless they were nurses or teachers). Yet in no way did I anticipate the adjustments I would need to make. We attended a small church where my husband was firmly established, having served as pastor for four years before I arrived. The members in that church were wonderful—and still keep in touch with us to this day—but things were running so smoothly that I didn't feel very needed. Still, I enjoyed being married and found plenty to do, developing more domestic skills for my new lifestyle and helping my husband in the parish.

It was when our first child, Rick, was born that I hit rock bottom. Rick had colic for six months; he cried day and night. I have laugh-ingly said that he didn't sleep during the night until he was seven years old—at least it seemed that long to me. No kind of milk or baby food was compatible with his digestive system. I felt frantic—and trapped. I began to see myself as I really was now that the "props" had been removed from my life. Before, I had been "propped up" by family, friends, a meaningful job, money to spend, and freedom to go wherever and whenever I chose. I had felt strong—almost invincible. But now that the props had been removed, I felt very insecure as a homemaker and as a new mom. I knew that I was powerless to overcome the situation on my own. I tried harder, but nothing worked. I was becoming the kind of person I despised—tired, irritable, unhappy, hopeless at times, and jealous of the fresh air and the adult conversations my husband enjoyed.

One morning, as Ralph left for work, I, in total frustration, said some very hurtful things to him. He was kind enough not to respond defensively, but I knew that I was at a crossroads in my marriage and my life. I went into our bedroom, knelt beside the unmade bed, and prayed the most sincere prayer of my life: "Lord, if you can do anything with this warped personality of mine, it is yours for as long as I live." No grand feelings of joy flooded my heart, but a deep sense of peace permeated my frustrated, fragmented inner being. That day I wrote in my spiritual journal: "Anytime you touch even the hem of his garment in desperate, believing faith, you too will be made whole."

I decided not to tell anybody about the experience. Three days later, my husband said, "Do you realize that you are singing for the first time in months?" Though my outer circumstances didn't change—Rick continued to cry, we didn't get an increase in salary so that we could hire babysitters more often, and my husband and I didn't have more time together—my inward state and my perspective of my world changed drastically.

My healing was not as instantaneous as Veronica's healing. After all, God had lots of personality kinks to work out in me—and still has some. But like Veronica's healing, my healing was certain. Since then my life has been "anchored," and my confidence has been in him "who is able to do exceedingly abundantly above all that we ask or think" (Ephesians 3:20 NKJV). Indeed, in the words of the popular William J. Gaither hymn: "The hand of Jesus touched me, and now I am no longer the same" ("He Touched Me," 1963).

Lesson 2: The simple certainty of faith enables us to dream and believe in ourselves.

Doris Christopher is an attractive, soft-spoken CEO who broke the glass ceiling without planning to do so. As a stay-at-home mom with two daughters, Doris began her company, The Pampered Chef, with an investment of $3,000 borrowed from an insurance policy. Through the years, the company has grown into a multimillion dollar corporation employing more than eleven hundred people at the home office in Addison, Illinois, and in three countries around the world.

What is The Pampered Chef, and what is the secret of the woman behind the company that *Inc.* magazine rated as one of the fastest growing privately held companies in America? On two occasions, I have had the opportunity to find answers to these questions. As a motivational speaker at the company's national conferences in Chicago and Toronto, I observed beautifully orchestrated sessions in which there was high energy, excitement, training, motivation, laughter, awards, and proposed incentive trips to Paris, Hawaii, and the Caribbean. The sessions were professionally produced with a smooth technological sophistication that rivaled a Hollywood production. A makeup artist and hairstylist were provided for each presenter, as well as separate dressing rooms. It is a first-class organization! These conferences, as well as regional ones, are designed to train and motivate the company's Kitchen Consultants (65,000 in the U.S., Canada, Germany, and the United Kingdom), who are the heart of the business.

How did it all begin? I had the privilege of interviewing Doris Christopher, the woman behind the company's success. She is easy to be with and has the gift of putting others at ease. Doris has both quiet charm and straightforward common sense.

Born in Oak Lawn, Illinois, a suburb of Chicago, Doris was the youngest of three daughters in a middle-class Lutheran family, which was firmly steeped in a strong work ethic. She graduated from the University of Illinois at Champaign-Urbana with a degree in home economics and worked for several years with the University Cooperative Extension. When she and her husband had children, Doris became a stay-at-home mom. As the girls got older, she began to think of some part-time wage earning opportunities that could utilize her skills and talents.

At first, she thought of catering, but she discarded that idea when she realized that catering would take her away from her family on weekends and holidays. In 1989, with the help and support of her husband and the encouragement of their daughters, Doris developed the idea for The Pampered Chef. The idea was simple: sell good quality kitchen and food preparation items directly to customers through actual cooking demonstrations in real kitchens. That year, the first kitchen show was held with Doris as the only consultant. By the end of the year, the company had $50,000 in sales. Today, the 65,000 consultants have sales reaching more than $700 million.

Doris recognized the entrepreneurial power of women and the growing trend of women leaving the full-time workforce and opting for a work-family split that favors home-based employment. Hers was an idea whose time had come.

In his "Trend Letter," John Naisbitt suggested that the ascendancy of the mall is over because of the competition from many home-based retailers that add a personal touch to their products. He also indicated that the ultimate in personal touch is The Pampered Chef, which sells household goods within the home.

What is the recipe for success given by the dynamic CEO of The Pampered Chef? In Doris's words, the recipe is to combine equal amounts of hard work, concentration, and vision with family togetherness, faith, and commitment, to mix well, and then to thrive.

As I listened to Doris on the day of our interview, I became convinced that her success came from a deeply ingrained Christian faith given to her by her family and her church. This faith enabled her to believe in herself and the possibilities before her. Just as the nameless woman with the issue of blood took a leap of faith to believe that Jesus could heal her, so also Doris Christopher took a leap of faith to begin her business. With faith, we, too, can do great things.

Lesson 3: A touch from Christ can enable us to overcome unimaginable difficulties and tragedies.

It is hard for me to imagine the difficulties that this unnamed woman with the issue of blood must have suffered because of her circumstances. Yet she overcame them because of her faith in Christ. Millions of people through the centuries have done the same thing. One such person is my friend June Scobee Rodgers. June was married to Dick Scobee, commander of the ill-fated *Challenger Seven* space shuttle, which exploded only seconds after take-off on January 28, 1986. Today, she is married to retired Lt. Gen. Don Rodgers, who lost his first wife to cancer some years ago. The horrible experience of watching replay after replay of her husband's space shuttle explode in midair via constant television coverage is only one of the many difficulties this remarkable woman has overcome through her rock-solid faith.

Before I tell of her early struggles, let me describe "Junebug"— a term affectionately given her by Don Rodgers and picked up by some of her friends. She is an extremely pretty woman who is always smartly dressed and gracious in manner. She has authentic charm—a mixture of graciousness, competence, sensitivity to people, and a delightful sense of humor. June is a speaker and the author of two books. One is a coffee-table book about the history of Chattanooga, Tennessee; the other is titled *Silver Linings: Triumph of the* Challenger Seven (Macon, Ga.: Peake Road, 1996) which tells the story of the shuttle's explosion and the events thereafter. The latter includes a foreword written by Dr. Robert Schuller and endorsements by Senator John Glenn and former President George Bush.

June's strength for turning tragedy into triumph and problems into possibilities began early in her life. Her victorious spirit was encouraged through understanding teachers and a minister who introduced June to the Christian faith and helped her believe with Paul: "I can do everything through him who gives me strength" (Philippians 4:13 NIV). Her own bright mind and determination contributed to her ability to overcome.

June grew up in poverty in rural Alabama. She says that when people compare their stories of poverty, she always wins. Her father, an itinerant carpenter, loved his family but had difficulty finding enough employment to provide well for them. Her mother was hospitalized from time to time for mental and emotional illnesses. This left June, the oldest child, the responsibility of caring for the home and her younger brothers.

As schoolchildren often do, June's classmates teased her and her brothers about the clothes they wore and the house in which they lived. One incident she remembers vividly hangs on the wall of her memories. The sixth grade teacher asked each of the students to tell the class what they would like to be when they grew up. When it was June's turn, she said, "I want to be a teacher." One girl laughed and called out, "You're so poor, you'll never see the inside of a college." Though the remark was embarrassing, it also crystallized June's dream and filled her with determination.

June not only graduated from college but also received two graduate degrees, including a Ph.D. from Texas A & M University. In addition to teaching in public schools and at the university level, she served on the President's National Advisory Council. A number of years ago when Alabama observed "June Scobee Day," June was able to include some guests in the festivities. Among them was the woman who, as a sixth grader, had made the humiliating but dream-crystallizing remark.

On January 28, 1986, when her heart and her dreams exploded like *Challenger Seven* into a million pieces, it was the miraculous touch of Christ that enabled her to go on and eventually triumph. She has been the "sparkplug" in the creation of the forty-three Challenger Space Centers for science education in the U.S. and England. June concludes her inspirational book *Silver Linings* with these words: "Only through a closer walk with our Savior Jesus Christ can we have the courage to boldly walk along the path that teaches us the lessons we need in the school of life" (p. 114).

Whatever our circumstances may be, life can be difficult. Your own life may be filled with problems and seemingly insurmountable difficulties. The primary lesson we learn from the woman with the issue of blood is this: It was her faith in Jesus Christ that made her strong. With his power, we can overcome!

Digging a Little Deeper

1. Read Luke 8:43-47, the story of the woman with the issue of blood. After suffering for twelve years and finding no help from physicians, why do you think she might have thought that this traveling teacher, of whom she perhaps had never heard, could help her? Discuss.

2. Now read Mark's version of the story (Mark 5:25-34). Compare and contrast the two accounts. Why do you think Luke, the physician, did not include in his account this detail recorded by Mark: "Yet instead of getting better she grew worse" (5:26 NIV)? Discuss.

3. Read Luke 8:46. How did Jesus know that someone had touched him in faith?

4. Why do you think that being anchored by faith in Christ enables us to believe more easily in ourselves?

5. Recall a "touch of Jesus" in your own life that was life changing. Write about the experience in your spiritual journal or discuss it with your group.

6. In what following areas do you believe Christ is calling you?

   • triumphing over a difficult circumstance. Describe.
   • embracing a new dream. What is the dream?
   • seeing a recent ending in your life, such as changing careers, moving to a new city and leaving family and friends behind, or losing a loved one.

7.

Priscilla

A Servant Leader with a Keen Mind and a Loving Heart

Scripture Text: **Acts 18:1-3, 18, 24-26; Romans 16:3-4**

After this, Paul left Athens and went to Corinth. There he met a Jew named Aquila, a native of Pontus, who had recently come from Italy with his wife Priscilla, because Claudius had ordered all the Jews to leave Rome. Paul went to see them, and because he was a tentmaker as they were, he stayed and worked with them.

—Acts 18:1-3 NIV

Priscilla's Story

Moriah tried to persuade her daughter, Priscilla, to go outside to play on the warm days in Rome. But the child practically hadn't stopped reading since her father first taught her when she was seven. "She has the mind of a scholar, and it would be a shame to waste it," he explained each time his wife questioned the wisdom of educating a girl in their culture. "She has a zest for learning and is as interested in mathematics as in the scriptures."

Priscilla's mother began to feel better about things as she watched her daughter grow into a lovely young woman who reached out to others in love and compassion. Priscilla's high standards of morality came from her knowledge and belief in the Jewish religious law. There were a number of suitors for Priscilla, but none seemed to interest her until Aquila, the young man from Pontus, came into her life. He, too, was Jewish and somewhat scholarly, though much more quiet and reserved than the friendly, outgoing, and enthusiastic Priscilla. Aquila's trade was tentmaking, and he was well employed by a company in Rome.

Priscilla's parents could see the young couple's friendship growing into love. Their only concern was Aquila's interest in the new Christian sect. Over her parents' objections, Priscilla began to attend some of the meetings. Her inquisitive mind always caused her to seek the truth about God. It was she, before Aquila, who became convinced that Jesus was the Messiah.

"I told you that a girl just shouldn't be thinking about theological matters," Moriah said to her husband one day. "Why, she may even end up being one of those itinerant preachers."

Her husband laughed uproariously and replied, "Well, she would make a good one." Then, seeing the look of fear and genuine anxiety on his wife's face, he added solemnly, "Don't worry, Moriah. That girl has a good head on her shoulders. She's not only smart, but wise as well."

Perhaps Priscilla's parents might have fought her on the issue if the Emperor Claudius hadn't decided suddenly to expel all Jews from Rome. It was a time of terrible turmoil, and Aquila and Priscilla were a steadying force for all their people, helping each one decide logically where to go. In fact, there was so much peace and love and power in the lives of Priscilla and Aquila that her parents became convinced this new faith must be from God. Before the dispersion, they quickly planned a simple but beautiful wedding for the young couple. Aquila and Priscilla would be going to Corinth, where Aquila would continue his tentmaking business. They tried diligently to persuade Priscilla's parents to go with them, but the latter chose to locate closer to Rome, hoping someday to return to their home.

———————

The preceding drama, though drawn from my imagination, serves as a prelude to the biblical story of Priscilla. We learn in the book of Acts that soon after Aquila and Priscilla moved from Italy to the seaport town of Corinth, which was noted for its immorality and wickedness, they met the apostle Paul. Since Paul, too, was a tentmaker, he worked with the young couple, lived in their home for eighteen months, and established a Christian church there (Acts 18:1-4).

I can imagine how Priscilla must have thrilled at hearing the stories of the Resurrection and Pentecost, which had been told to Paul by Peter and the other apostles, as well as the stories of Paul's own experience on the road to Damascus. He also told Priscilla and Aquila of the adventures of his missionary journeys, which he had undertaken for the seemingly impossible task of winning the world for Christ.

Paul's enthusiasm was contagious, and his power in preaching became the model for Priscilla's own articulate presentation of the gospel. In addition, Paul's leadership skills honed her own. These skills, in combination with her natural tact, fine mind, and great love of people made her a forceful influence in the early church. God was preparing a woman for quiet but mighty leadership.

The reason for this preparation soon became apparent. When Paul left Corinth, he sailed for Ephesus, taking with him Aquila and Priscilla to establish the Christian church there (Acts 18:18). Their success is evident in Paul's letter to the church at Ephesus.

Soon after Paul's departure for Antioch, another preacher appeared at Ephesus. He was Apollos from Alexandria, a learned man and a dynamic communicator (Acts 18:24-25). The problem was that he didn't know the whole truth; he knew the story of Jesus only through the baptism of John. He didn't know about the Resurrection or the power of the indwelling presence of the risen Christ in the believer's life. So Aquila and Priscilla invited Apollos to their home and gave him the whole story (Acts 18:26). The fact that he learned these new truths and became even more powerful in his preaching is a tribute to his humil-ity and to the tact of Aquila and Priscilla.

Priscilla and her husband were not only organizers but also encouragers of others. They remained close friends of Paul, and he expressed his gratitude to them in Romans 16:3-4: "Greet Priscilla and Aquila, my fellow workers in Christ Jesus. They risked their lives for me. Not only I but all the churches of the Gentiles are grateful to them" (NIV).

In the book *All of the Women of the Bible* (New York: Harper and Bros., 1955), Edith Deen indicates that not only scripture but also historical records attest to Priscilla's fame as a preacher and a leader (p. 229). Her name in Rome was *Prisca*. One of the old-est catacombs in Rome bears her name, and a church on the Aventine was named for her. Likewise, in the tenth century, there was a popular legendary writing entitled "Acts of St. Prisca."

Priscilla was indeed a Christian leader because she used her keen mind and her loving heart to serve Christ. We, too, can be servant leaders in every facet of our lives if we place our minds and hearts under the control of Christ.

What Can We Learn from Priscilla?

Lesson 1: Those who have wisdom use their minds without conceit and without seeking to dominate others.

There is a difference between knowledge and wisdom. Webster's *New World Dictionary* defines knowledge as "a mental grasp of a body of facts." In contrast, the definition of wisdom is "the power of judging rightly and following the soundest course of action, based on knowledge, experience, and understanding."

Solomon's prayer before he ascended to the throne of Israel to succeed his father, King David, is one of the most beautiful in the Bible. The request he made is this: "So give your servant a discerning heart to govern your people and to distinguish between right and wrong" (1 Kings 3:9 NIV). In the following verses, we learn that God was pleased by Solomon's request and replied, "I will give you a wise and discerning heart" (v. 12 NIV).

Among the spiritual gifts listed in 1 Corinthians 12:8-11 and 1 Corinthians 13, the greatest, I believe, are wisdom and love. Without them, the others don't have the same power. For example, the gifts of teaching, preaching, and even hospitality can be shallow and superficial without wisdom and love. These are the two gifts for which I most yearn, because only with these gifts can we find and live out "the most excellent way" to which Paul refers (1 Corinthians 12:31 NIV).

Priscilla definitely had the gifts of wisdom and love in abundance. One evidence of this was her ability to help the popular speaker Apollos. Such a powerful speaker who received great adulation might have resented someone—especially a woman—having the audacity to correct his message (Acts 18:24-26). Understanding this dynamic, and knowing that the gospel message could be diluted if Apollos stopped the story with the water baptism by John, gave Priscilla the courage and confidence to confront Apollos. Yet she knew she had to confront him with wisdom, love, and great humility of spirit. James 3:13 tells us that if we are truly wise, then our deeds will be done in humility.

Another evidence of Priscilla's wisdom and love was that she never used her keen mind to show conceit or to dominate others. One example is the happy and pleasant relationship she had with her husband, Aquila. Most scholars say that it was unheard of in that day for a wife's name to be listed ahead of her husband's. Yet in the six times they are mentioned in scripture, three times her name is listed first. Many husbands in that culture would have been "out of there" in no time flat! It was Priscilla's respect and love for Aquila, coupled with her tact and kindness, that allowed him to follow her leadership without feeling inferior.

There also is evidence of Priscilla's wisdom and love in her relationship with the apostle Paul. For some people, the name Paul is synonymous with a dislike of women. In fairness, we need to remember the number of women he invited to help in his ministry, including Lydia, Phebe, and Priscilla. My guess is that most women of his day didn't have educational opportunities; nor did they have Paul's leadership skills and singleness of purpose. Perhaps Paul didn't dislike women but found most to be unable to fulfill the tremendously urgent tasks of winning both Jew and Gentile for Christ and of establishing Christian churches throughout the world. For him, it was a magnificent obsession—and we can be thankful that it was.

Priscilla was certainly a woman whom Paul respected and trusted—along with her husband—to carry on the work in Corinth and to establish the church in Ephesus. Paul sent special greetings to them in several of his letters, and he thanked them profusely in his letter to the Romans for their help (16:3-4).

Today, women hold leadership positions in almost every segment of our society—education, health care, the military, religion, politics, athletics, communications, and business. A number of them have made a difference on the world stage, including Golda Meir, prime minister of Israel from 1969 to 1974; Indira Gandhi, prime minister of India from 1960 to 1984; Margaret Thatcher, prime minister of Great Britain from 1979 to 1990; and Madeline Albright, United States delegate to the United Nations from 1993 to 1996 and U.S. secretary of state from 1996 to 2001.

The women in leadership roles who have made a difference for good are those who have led or currently are leading with true wisdom. They have helped to create harmony, not chaos; trust, not deceit; and hope, not despair.

On a personal level, there are two wonderful women who have impressed me greatly with their wisdom. One is Ruth Street, a widow who seems ageless and is a member of the same church as I. She is a woman of impeccable dress, manners, and material wealth who has supported all the ministries of her church and countless other causes in the name of Christ. Her financial support is also generous to worthy community activities too numerous to mention. But her greatest wealth can be found in her inner qualities of graciousness, generosity of spirit, faith, humor, thoughtfulness, and love of people. An evidence of how people reciprocate her love can be found in the long line of people— from teenagers to senior adults—who wait in our church's narthex every Sunday after worship to speak to her and give her a hug. She has wisely used her mind and her position of influence to further the cause of Christ in our world.

The second woman who has impressed me greatly with her wisdom is my mother-in-law, the late Clarine Mohney. According to today's standards, she, having only a high school education, would not be considered a well-educated woman. Yet she was one of the most knowledgeable women I have ever known. She was well read, especially in the fields that interested her: music, poetry, flowers, religion, and health. More important, she was a wise woman with a heart full of love for people and for Christ. She taught Sunday school, arranged flowers each week for worship, visited and helped persons who were ill or shut in, and with her husband, tithed their income, a practice passed on to each of their four sons.

My mother-in-law was always eager to come and help, if asked, when a new baby was born or when there was an illness in the family. Because of her sensitivity to people's needs, hopes, and dreams, her advice was wise. Yet she never got upset if the advice wasn't followed. I appreciated her Christian faith more than any of her other attributes. She had a bedrock faith in Jesus Christ, and she evidenced it in positive, "can do" attitudes and acts of love. She truly believed with the apostle Paul that "those three remain: faith, hope, and love. But the greatest of these is love" (1 Corinthians 13:13 NIV).

Through the centuries, countless women have followed the example of Priscilla by using their minds without conceit and without seeking to dominate others. They have chosen loving wisdom over knowledge. Wisdom and love make an unbeatable combination for Christian faith. Just as this winning combination helped Priscilla and Aquila "grow the church" in Corinth and Ephesus, as well as train Apollos, so also it can help us today—in our personal relationships and in our churches. Wisdom enables us to see clearly and to make correct judgments; love allows us to do both with humility and in the spirit of our Lord. May we, too, follow Priscilla's example of servant leadership by choosing to live in wisdom and love.

Lesson 2: *A strong husband and wife team can have an effective ministry.*

Over the years, I have been aware of the number of couples in the same profession whose marriages have ended in divorce—in Hollywood, in television, in business, in medicine, and even in Christian ministry. Part of the reason may be hectic schedules that collide and leave little time for cultivating personal relationships. In addition to this hindrance, there often are power struggles based on selfishness and conflicting egos. Priscilla and Aquila give us a wonderful example of teamwork. In scripture they usually are mentioned together. There is no evidence that one tried to control the other. They were not unequally yoked but were united in their belief in Christ. Evidently they made a covenant to "accomplish together" from the hour of their marriage. Theirs was a unity of purpose and spirit. They were one in their service to Christ.

It was Paul who discovered this amazing pair. Acts 18:2 says, "he [Paul] met a Jew named Aquila . . . with his wife Priscilla" (NIV). What a find! Both were already schooled in Old Testament scriptures; but with Paul—the early church's greatest Bible teacher—as their houseguest for eighteen months, they must have received a marvelous theological education. Their preparation was now complete; and when the call came to serve in Corinth and in Ephesus, they didn't hesitate to go—together.

Priscilla and Aquila also were one in their secular work. No doubt Aquila learned the tent trade when he was young. Rabbis of that day thought that if a father failed to teach his son a trade, he was teaching him to be a thief (Lockyer, *All the Women of the Bible,* Grand Rapids: Zondervan, 1967, p. 123). Priscilla helped Aquila in the business, thus making them teammates in vocation (I can only hope that in the home he also helped her with the dishes and the housework!). In their tent making, I believe we can assume two things. First, their work glorified God because of its excellence. No Christian should do slipshod work because it reflects negatively on the One we serve. The second assumption is that they had the opportunity to speak persuasively of their faith, even inviting customers, if they showed interest, to the church that met in their home. Together, they were an effective ministry team!

Priscilla and Aquila set a very high standard for Christian husband and wife relationships. From my experience, I've learned that marital teamwork, which looks so effortless for them, does not always come easily. Perhaps they didn't have children, which we parents know bring brand new possibilities for stress and struggles! In any case, effective teamwork is hammered out on the anvil of joy and sorrow, pain and happiness, problems and solutions. It involves respect, trust, commitment, communication, laughter, fun, faith, love, and forgiveness on the part of *both* spouses. And it always means that both husband and wife must be flexible and willing to grow and change.

My husband, Ralph, and I have learned to be an effective team, but it has been a continuing process. I was very insecure in my early marriage—about my personal appearance; about my roles as a wife, a minister's wife, and later a parent; and about my ability to cook, entertain, and speak publicly. It was Ralph who "affirmed" me into confidence. He would say things such as, "You look great today! That color looks good on you." He encouraged our hospitality to friends and groups from the church by helping to entertain. He also affirmed my first feeble efforts at public speaking to adults. And when invitations began to come for me to speak to groups, he encouraged me to take them. Of course, there was one thing he couldn't honestly affirm, and that was my cooking! But through time and necessity, I learned.

Through the years, Ralph and I have learned from each other. He learned the art of affirmation and communication, and I learned the subtle art of Christian assertiveness (for Ralph is a "take charge" guy). We also learned that the closer we grow to Christ as individuals, the closer we grow to each other. Today, Ralph is as supportive in my speaking and writing ministry as I was in his parish ministry.

In the future, whether or not we are in active ministry, Ralph and I continually will need to grow and change and learn in our efforts to be an effective team. You see, you don't have to be in professional ministry in order to be an effective "ministry team." In fact, *every* Christian married couple can be an effective team.

Lesson 3: The home is a valuable tool for evangelism.

If we are not winsome witnesses in our own homes, then we will be superficial witnesses elsewhere. This is really where the "rubber meets the road"—and it is not easy.

How well I remember one day when our children were small—four and six years of age. I left the church, where I had been complimentary and kind to the women in my group, and I went home and exploded over the fact that the children had tracked mud onto a freshly mopped floor. It was the look of hurt in my younger son's eyes that caused me to put my head on the table and weep. I asked for God's forgiveness, as well as for my sons' forgiveness, which they readily gave. Incidentally, they taught me something that day about accepting forgiveness from God and others. I felt so terrible about my actions that I kept trying to earn the forgiveness I had already received. When they went outside to play, I took a special toy out to them; and a little later, I took them milk and cookies. At this point, Rick, the six-year-old, said, "You don't have to keep bringing things out to us, Mother. We have already forgiven you."

Later that day, I wondered if those little boys would want to know the Christ I served and would seek to live with any of my values, or if they would go in opposite directions. That day was a turning point for me. This doesn't mean that I never got upset again. I did. I also needed our sons' forgiveness a number of times in the future. But that day, I began to understand the danger of unreasonable anger, and I began to work on my own anger. I wholeheartedly believe what I once heard Dr. Elton Trueblood, a Quaker author and professor, say in a sermon: "The family is the Kingdom of God in miniature."

Priscilla showed us another way the home can play a role in winning others for Christ. She and Aquila opened their homes in Corinth and in Ephesus so that the church could meet there. In Paul's letter to the Corinthians, he wrote: "Aquila and Priscilla greet you warmly in the Lord, and so does the church that meets at their house" (1 Corinthians 16:19 NIV). Likewise, in the letter to the Romans, Paul sent his greetings to them and to "the church that meets at their house" (16:5 NIV). Because of poverty and persecution in those days, separate buildings for worship were impractical. House churches became the places to worship God.

Even today, there are Bible studies held in homes. In our neighborhood, there is a Bible study group that meets on Tuesday mornings, and so many cars are parked on one particular street from 10:00 A.M. until noon that you can hardly drive down the street. I am convinced that many people who are uncomfortable inside a church will go without hesitation to a friend's home for a study of "the greatest story ever told."

Priscilla and Aquila gave us the pattern for this kind of evangelism. Will we follow their example?

Digging a Little Deeper

1. Read Acts 18:1-4 and 18-19. What do these verses tell us about Priscilla's involvement in the emerging Christian faith? Why was it so unusual for a woman to be a church leader at this time? Discuss.

2. In 1 Corinthians 11:5, Paul talks of women praying and prophesying in church. Yet in 1 Corinthians 14:34-35, he seems to be contradicting himself. How so? Consult a study Bible or Bible commentary to find a possible explanation for this seeming contradiction. Discuss. Why, then, should we not be surprised that Paul encouraged women such as Lydia and Phebe to work in his ministry?

3. What evidences can you find in the scriptures to suggest that Priscilla was wise and tactful? Discuss. Tell of a wise Christian you know.

4. In James 3:13, we read that if we are truly wise, then our deeds will be done in humility. Why is humility an important part of wisdom?

5. How do we know that Paul was grateful for the work of Aquila

and Priscilla? Read Romans 16:3-4. How do you think this written appreciation made the couple feel? How do *you* feel when you receive appreciation for a job well done—and when you don't? Discuss.

6. In what ways were Aquila and Priscilla a great husband and wife team? Discuss.

7. Tell of a great Christian husband and wife team you know personally. How would you rate the "harmony" and "oneness" of their marriage? Regardless of their chosen professions, in what ways are they an effective "team" for Christ?

8. If you are married, discuss the following questions privately with your spouse: How would you describe the current stage or state of your marriage? What changes do you need to make—as individuals and as a couple—to improve your relationship? How can you be an effective team for Christ?

9. How did Priscilla and Aquila use their home as a tool for evangelism? How can you use your home to reach and serve others for Christ? Discuss.

8.

Lydia

She Wanted Significance,
Not Just Success

Scripture Text: **Acts 16:14-15**

One of those listening was a woman named Lydia, a dealer in purple cloth from the city of Thyatira, who was a worshiper of God. The Lord opened her heart to respond to Paul's message.

—Acts 16:14 NIV

Lydia's Story

Note: Some of the details in the following story, including Lydia's physical description, are drawn from my imagination in order to paint a more complete, colorful picture of Lydia than is given in the biblical text.

Lydia was a standout in the city of Philippi in every way. Her personal appearance turned heads as she walked down the streets of that Roman colony, the most prosperous city in the province of Macedonia. She was a tall, stately woman with dark hair and "laughing eyes." In addition, she always wore purple. It was extremely becoming to her, and it also was good for business, for she was a "dealer in purple cloth" (Acts 16:14). The cloth had been dyed from a secretion of shellfish, the mollusk (William Barclay, *The Acts of the Apostles,* Philadelphia: Westminster Press, 1955, p. 133). The secretion was clear in the veins of the shellfish; but when exposed to sunlight, it turned a royal purple or a crimson red. People of wealth and royalty bought the purple fabric; but *every* woman, whatever her economic status, longed and saved for at least one such garment before she died.

Perhaps Lydia was most outstanding because she was a liberated woman who owned and successfully operated her own business. This was extremely rare even in a Roman colony. Actually, Lydia had not grown up in Philippi but in Thyatira in Asia Minor (Herbert Lockyer, *All the Women of the Bible,* Grand Rapids: Zondervan Publishing, 1967, p. 84). Most scholars believe that she had been married and had left Thyatira after her husband's death. It was then that she had moved to Philippi.

In that Roman colony, she became known as a competent and very respected businesswoman with obvious wealth. She must have had a spacious home with servants in order for Paul, Silas, and their entourage to stay there. Her home also became the meeting place of the first Christian church in that city (Acts 16:40).

When I think of Lydia and her many accomplishments, the following attributes come to mind: vision, enthusiasm, hospitality, focus, and mental acumen. Yet with all that, there was something missing in her life. Perhaps she recognized that this void was more than her loneliness caused by the death of her husband and her move to a new city. Perhaps she also saw that her Jewish customers were anchored in a strong belief in the One True God. One of the Jewish women who met on the banks of the Gangites River each Sabbath to pray and study must have seen that Lydia was "searching" and thus invited her to join them. According to some authorities, Lydia became a regular member of the group. In the book *All of the Women of the Bible* (New York: Harper and Bros., 1955), Edith Deen writes: "It can be assumed that this little prayer group of which Lydia was a member had asked for guidance, and Paul had been sent to them for a great purpose, because they were receptive to the truth" (p. 223). I am convinced that when we pray with sincerity, expectancy, and a searching heart, God will move heaven and earth to give us the help we need!

Meanwhile, the apostle Paul was in Troas. He had not planned to go to Macedonia, but then he had had a dream in which a man begged him to "come over to Macedonia and help us" (Acts 16:9 NIV). Paul considered this a nudge from God, so he and his entourage left for Philippi, the capital city of Macedonia.

It was there, on the banks of the Gangites, that Paul found the small group of women. When he preached to them about the risen Christ, of whom I assume they had never heard, his message found instant lodging in Lydia's heart. She became the first European Christian convert, and she was baptized in the Gangites. That very day, Lydia invited Paul and his group to stay in her home as long as they were in town.

It was to this band of believers that Paul wrote his letter to the Philippians, which has been described as a love letter of joy. He opens the letter with these wonderful words: "I thank my God every time I remember you" (Philippians 1:3 NIV).

Lydia exemplifies the independence some women of Asia Minor had achieved in her day. But more important for us Christians, she was the first European convert to Christianity. She will be remembered as the one who picked up the torch from Paul at Philippi and carried it steadfastly.

What Can We Learn from Lydia?

Lesson 1: When we earnestly seek, we will find.

In Matthew 7:7, Jesus promised: "Ask and it will be given to you; seek and you will find; knock and the door will be opened to you" (NIV). This was true for Lydia. Despite beauty, wealth, friends, and business success, Lydia felt an emptiness in her life. It was on the river bank that Lydia began to find the "something more" for which she had been searching.

Back in Lydia's native city of Thyatira, the deity was Apollo, the sun god. But in the midst of her life's transitions, that god had no answers. He could not promise eternal life as did Jesus: "I am the resurrection and the life. Those who believe in me, even though they die, will live" (John 11:25). Nor could Apollo give the promise of the gift of the Holy Spirit, which Jesus gave to assure us that we would not be left comfortless: "And I will ask the Father, and he will give you another Counselor to be with you forever—the Spirit of truth. The world cannot accept him, because it neither sees him nor knows him. But you know him, for he lives with you and will be in you" (John 14:15-17 NIV).

A number of years ago, a beautiful young woman who lived in a world of inordinate wealth said to me: "I have everything that most people feel would make them happy, and I am miserable." She was in a very unhappy marriage, and she had sought help from a high-priced counselor for years. The "something more" she needed was an authentic relationship with Jesus Christ, but she didn't believe that. All she wanted was someone to say some magic words and make her husband love her. Unfortunately, the marriage ended shortly after the conversation in which she had admitted her unhappiness. Now, some twenty years later, she still is searching for someone with a magic word to "fix" her former husband.

Unlike Lydia, this wealthy woman hasn't found the "something more" that gives life meaning. She has seen people who radiate the love and joy she longs for, but she refuses to believe that they have received their empowerment from the risen Christ. Despite elegant homes, world travel, beautiful clothes, and several face lifts, her heart is restless—and will remain so unless, as

Augustine said, she can believe that "you [God] made us for yourself and our hearts find no peace until they rest in you" (trans. R. S. Pyne-Coffin, *Confessions of St. Augustine,* Baltimore: Penguin Books, 1961, p. 21).

Lydia and the group of Jewish women who met on the banks of the Gangites sought help and guidance from God. Their prayers were answered. God sent Paul and Silas to enable them to find the "something more" that their hearts desired. Even if we have been believers for years, we continually need someone who will give our faith a boost and help us find "something more" that our lives may need. It may be a minister, a neighbor, a friend, a chance encounter with a complete stranger, or a family member.

Recently our nineteen-year-old granddaughter was home from college for spring break. "Gran, let's 'hang out' together tomorrow," she said in her usual cheery telephone voice. We do this often when she is in town, and I never come away from our time together without feeling renewed in spirit by this vivacious, enthusiastic young Christian. Even when I'm not intentionally "seeking" something from God, he often surprises me with a delightful "treasure." How blessed we are when we condition ourselves to seek God in all the moments, all the places, and all the people of our lives. We will find "immeasurably more than all we ask or imagine" (Ephesians 3:20 NIV).

Lesson 2: Wealth can either diminish our service to Christ or enlarge it.

All of us have some form of wealth—talents, influence, or material possessions. We may not feel that we have the latter, but in comparison with people in third world countries, we are rich in possessions. How we use this wealth is our choice.

Wealth of talent can diminish our service to Christ by leading us into egotism and pride; or if we choose, we can use our talents as spiritual gifts to build up the body of Christ and serve others in his name. On the one hand, wealth of influence can cause us to be power hungry—to be in power struggles with those in business, community, and even church and family. On the other hand, we can build others up, rejoice in their successes, share honors, and build teamwork. As for material wealth, we can use it to display our success and feed our desire for pleasure or our "need" for more possessions. Or like Lydia did, we can use all our resources—our possessions and talents and influence—to reach out in hospitality and service for Christ. The choice is ours!

When I think of the history of the Christian church, I think of the enormous amount of good that has been accomplished by those who either have renounced their wealth or have used it in an unselfish, generous fashion. Take Francis of Assisi, for example, who was born in 1182 into a family of great material wealth in Assisi, Italy. As a young man, he lived as a socialite who enjoyed the party scene. It was a chance encounter with a leper and his own serious illness that caused Francis to renounce his possessions, become a priest, and later establish the Franciscan Order of the Roman Catholic Church. He died in 1226, and in 1228, Francis was canonized by Pope Gregory IX for his work and service to others in the name of Christ (*New Catholic Encyclopedia,* Vol. VI, Washington, D.C.: Catholic University of America Press, 1967, pp. 28-29).

I think also of Florence Nightingale, who was born into an extremely wealthy British home. Interestingly, she was born during a family vacation in Florence, Italy—hence her name. As a beautiful young woman, she was expected to be a lady of leisure—"to the manor born." Instead, she felt that she heard the voice of God calling her to serve those who were ill. After attending a nurse's institute in Germany, she returned to London as Superintendent of British Health Services. She is perhaps best remembered for the risks she took in working with the wounded in the Crimean War. Even though she spent the last years of her life as a semi-invalid, she still served as a consultant for British hospitals (*World Book Encyclopedia,* vol. 14, Chicago, Ill., 2001, pp. 420-21).

Then there is the example of a twentieth-century American family, the Sebastian Kresges, who used their wealth wisely for the purposes of God. Sebastian was reared in a strong Christian family. He followed the admonition of Methodism's founder, John Wesley: Earn all you can, save all you can, so that you can give all that you can (see sermon 50, "The Use of Money," in *The Works of John Wesley,* vol. 2, Nashville: Abingdon Press, 1985, pp. 263-80). Sebastian established a chain of Kresge five and ten cent stores. In 1924, he established the Kresge Foundation with $1.3 million. When he died in 1966, he had given away $60 million to tax-exempt colleges and universities, which awarded bachelor's and master's degrees. The Kresge Foundation continues today.

In the midsixties, when my husband, Ralph, was president of a church-related college, we got to know Stanley Kresge—who had taken his father's position in the company and the Foundation—and his wife, Dorothy. We needed a new building on our campus, and we sought a grant from the Kresge Foundation. The problem was that every other tax-exempt institution seemed to be sitting on the foundation's doorstep. It would be a long time before they even got to our request.

"Why don't we make it a matter of concentrated prayer?" I asked Ralph one morning. He agreed. Shortly thereafter, a minister friend, Dr. Frank Porter—then District Superintendent of the Johnson City, Tennessee, District of the Methodist Church—telephoned with a question: "How would you like to meet Stanley and Dorothy Kresge?" Frank had known nothing of the college's request for a grant or our decision of concentrated prayer.

A good friend of the Kresges was to speak at a district rally in Johnson City. Since the Kresges were en route from Florida to their home in Michigan, Dr. Porter asked if we could attend a dinner planned for the speaker. It was a small dinner party during which each of us told something of our own faith journeys. It was the most stimulating evening of spiritual conversation Ralph and I had experienced in years. What's more, the excellent choir from our college presented music for the rally. The college received the needed grant, and we gained a friendship with the Kresges that lasted until their deaths. Only God could have orchestrated that series of events.

In the book *The S. S. Kresge Story* (Steve Spilos, Racine, Wis.: Western Publishing Company, 1979), Stanley Kresge tells of becoming Chairman of the Foundation at the time of his father's death in 1966. He expressed his strong conviction, which was passed on to him by his parents and grandparents: "This world will not be greatly improved until and unless the teachings, experiences and spirit of Jesus Christ are more fully understood and applied in our lives and promoted throughout the land" (p. 332). That statement is still the basis of all donations made by the Kresge Foundation.

The same book also includes an incident that happened in 1953 when Stanley Kresge's father attended the dedication of Harvard's Graduate School of Business Administration. He gave the shortest speech in Harvard history when he arose and said: "I never made a dime talking," and he sat down. Stanley Kresge said that those six words characterized his father's character and business philosophy; his passion for economy; the importance of small things, such as the dime, in the evolution of his business; and his vision for big things, for each of those six words represented $375,000 given from the Kresge Foundation to the Graduate School of Business Administration at Harvard.

Through the centuries, countless Christians such as the Kresges have followed the example of Lydia in using their wealth for the purposes of God—all in the name of Christ. Whether our material wealth is small or large, we can contribute to the causes of Christ around the world by tithing our time, our talents, and our money.

Lesson 3: Because people are drawn to those who possess attributes they admire, we Christians are called to be magnets for Jesus Christ.

When I was thirteen, a counselor at a summer camp was just such a person for me. Libby was young, attractive, and athletic, and she could sing like an angel. She was everything I wanted to be but wasn't. She had the kind of winsome personality that drew people to her like bees to honey. One night, she led vespers at which she told us about her life. Her childhood and high school years had been far from idyllic. An alcoholic mother and a father who traveled during the week left Libby with more than her share of responsibility.

None of this made her bitter—only better. This was possible because, as an eighth grader, she had committed her life to Christ. A strong youth group with understanding counselors at her church gave her the support she needed to live out her faith. "You need friends who are Christians to encourage and support you on the journey," she told us.

During free time every afternoon, Libby was surrounded by campers seeking help with personal problems. I was in the group but said little because I was in a state of mild teenage rebellion. For years I had tried to be just like my older sister, who was "good" and very smart. When I couldn't be like her, I decided to be as different from her as possible. One of my first acts of rebellion was not to accept Christ or join the church. Yet as Libby had experienced— and Lydia and the women who gathered on the river bank—I could feel myself being drawn into the net of faith. It was the warmth and vivacity of Libby's personality that drew me to her and, through her, to the One to whom I could commit my life.

As I've reflected on that experience through the years, I have become aware of the power of personality to influence others for good or evil. What attributes do you radiate, and to what—or to Whom—does your life point others?

For several months, I have been aware of a young woman who sits in front of us in church. By reading the Ritual of Friendship, which is a notepad on which those sitting on each pew may register their attendance, she is aware of visitors and new members who sit around her; and she takes time to greet each of them warmly. From one person who joined our church as a result of her warmth and friendliness, I learned that Jan follows up with each of them by telephone. When I told Jan how much my husband and I appreciate what she is doing for Christ and the church, she replied, "I had no idea that anyone was aware of that." Neither are we aware that we are being observed. Our actions mirror our Christian faith—or the lack of it.

Digging a Little Deeper

1. Read Acts 16. From what we know about the business success of those who dealt in purple dye and fabrics in Lydia's day, why was it unusual for her to be such a merchant? Discuss.

2. Lydia, the first European convert to Christianity, was a Philippian. From the background material provided in this chapter and the details included in Acts 16:11-12, what do we know about the city of Philippi? Discuss.

3. What reasons do you think that Lydia, a Gentile, might have had for meeting with a group of Jewish women to study the Hebrew scriptures and to pray for guidance? Discuss.

4. When have you prayed for guidance—either alone or with a group? What happened? Discuss.

5. Reread Acts 16:7-10. How did God use Paul to answer the

women's prayers for guidance? At some point in your life, has God used a person or persons to answer an urgent prayer of yours? How have you been used to answer someone else's prayer? Discuss.

6. How did God use Lydia's talents, influence, and generosity to help spread the Christian faith? Discuss.

7. What are some of your talents? How are you using them to serve Christ?

8. How is God seeking to use you today in the spread of the Christian faith? Are you willing to be used, or are you resisting? Why? Reflect and/or discuss.

9. Describe a person you know whose very personality is a magnet to draw others to Christ.

10. Which of your personality traits draw others to you and, through you, to Christ? Which of your personality traits need improving? Discuss.

For the Journey Ahead

In this book, we have looked at the stories of eight New Testament women, including well-known women such as Mary, the devout teenage mother of the Son of God. Also included are nameless women, such as Peter's wife and the woman with the issue of blood. Yet the Christian attributes evident in each of these women are needed in our own day as much as in their day—attributes such as love, loyalty, wisdom, faith, courage, spirituality, and the fine art of "being" (not just doing). The following questions and suggestions are offered to help you cultivate these attributes in your own life:

1. Memorize and be inspired by the following Bible verses:

- Yet in all these things we are more than conquerors through Him who loved us. (Romans 8:37 NKJV)
- He who has begun a good work in you will complete it. (Philippians 1:6 NKJV)
- And now abide faith, hope, love, these three; but the greatest of these is love. (1 Corinthians 13:13 NKJV)
- The God of love and peace will be with you. (2 Corinthians 13:11 NKJV)
- Hope is the anchor of the soul. (Hebrews 6:19, author's paraphrase)
- My peace I give unto you: not as the world giveth, give I unto you. Let not your heart be troubled, neither let it be afraid. (John 14:27 KJV)
- I have come that they [you] may have life, and that they [you] may have it more abundantly. (John 10:10 NKJV)
- These things I have spoken to you, that my joy may remain in you, and that your joy may be full. (John 15:11 NKJV)
- Lo, I am with you always, even to the end of the age. (Matthew 28:20 NKJV)

2. Determine to make a difference in the lives of others in the name of Christ. This will include being sensitive to others, being kind, and being willing to serve rather than expecting to be served.
3. Make a thoughtful assessment of your talents and spirituals gifts, and see how you can best use them to "build up the body of Christ" (Ephesians 4:12). For example . . .

- If your gift is teaching, are you willing to sacrifice the time, energy, and caring necessary to teach biblical truths in interesting and relevant ways?
- If your gift is administration, are you willing to develop leadership skills so that in church and community undertak-

ings you may make a difference for God in the lives of others?

- If you have the gift of hospitality, are you showing warmth and encouragement to others wherever you see them—especially in church? Are you willing to open your home for meetings, Bible studies, and visits to welcome neighbors or new church members?

4. Is your faith being deepened daily through the study of God's word, prayer, worship (personal and communal), and service?
5. Is the enthusiasm, joy, courage, and devotion of these early Christian women evident in your life? Are these and other Christian attributes drawing people to you and, through you, to Christ?

May our Lord, who modeled these attributes while on earth, bless you on your journey and enable you to bless others!